Escaping Satan's Grasp

Will they survive?

❖

By Elizabeth Anne Phillips

DEDICATION

To ALMIGHTY GOD; Father, Son, and Holy Spirit with sincere gratitude for all You do.

To my sons, who, through their courage, saved lives by interfering with activities of the group who abused them.

To the many people who helped us in a multitude of ways. You know who you are.

TABLE OF CONTENTS

ACKNOWLEDGMENTS

IT HAS BEEN said that writing is a solitary endeavor, but I know there are many people involved with bringing a book to life.

With love and my undying gratitude, I want to thank Holy Spirit, my parents, and siblings, Kingdom Writers Association (especially Brae and Jill), my faithful critique group (Sarah, Jan, Tracy, and Liza), Sharon (my incredible cover artist) and Tiffany (my superlative editor, counselor, teacher, and friend), and my beta-readers (Jen, Michelle, Judy, Barbara, Tracy, Sarah, Sande, Cindy).

Thank you to the many people who prayed to bring this project to life.

And to you, dear Reader, may the story bring you freedom and help. May God bless you with courage, strength, and love.

Elizabeth Anne Phillips

INTRODUCTION

THE STORY YOU'RE about to read is a recounting of events I lived through in the early 1980s. Names and identifying details have been changed to protect both the innocent and the guilty.

Hopefully, by telling my story, I can save other victims before it is too late.

The occurrences in the physical realm are all true and actually happened.

My purpose in telling our story is to raise awareness. Abuse occurs in several forms, including generational Satanism.

How did I discover that the inconceivable, unbelievable, horrific events that had happened to my children actually occurred? How did I learn about spiritual warfare and how to navigate the real court system? Was I eventually able to protect my children from further abuse?

Looking back on those events, I imagine there were spiritual forces fighting both for and against me and my loved ones. I see them with great clarity. So, I have interspersed my retelling of my family's story with what I imagine might have been happening in the unseen world along the way. This spiritual realm affects our day-to-day lives far more than we realize, especially when we're in the midst of struggles.

The machinations and conversations going on in the demonic

parts of the spiritual realm must, of necessity, be conjecture from the imagination of the author.

After twenty years, I found peace and forgave my ex-husband for his heinous involvement.

Yes, I forgave him.

I realized that he, too, is a victim. Many abusers were themselves abused as children. This is especially true in multigenerational occult sects.

Forgiving doesn't mean forgetting what happened or providing opportunities for abuse to happen again. Forgiveness means allowing God to handle the offense and giving up my perceived right to vengeance. And that forgiveness didn't happen overnight; it was and is a process. Like peeling an onion, it involves lots of layers, lots of tears, and lots of time. But it is worth it. Forgiveness freed my family—it freed me.

If you're reading this because you've experienced anything like this, I'm with you. There are no words for the unfathomable terror of trying to protect your child from abuse. And forgiveness is probably the farthest thing from your mind. But I believe you will get there. Why? Because God loves you and those you love more than you can ever imagine. And because in the end…God wins!

So, with respect and honor to C.S. Lewis, author of *The Screwtape Letters* and Frank Peretti, author of *This Present Darkness* who have both inspired me in many ways, here is my story.

Escaping Satan's Grasp

Will they survive?

CHAPTER 1

MIRE SHOOK WITH fear, small particles of ash falling from his stumpy, sooty wings. He nervously fingered the crystal hanging around his neck.

"Inventory report!" growled the deep, menacing voice of his commanding officer. "And it had better have improved since the last time! The master wants a good selection to choose from for this offering."

"Yes, milord. We have two teenage runaways and three breeders ready to be delivered."

"Is that all?!" his superior roared. As he turned on his subordinate, his wings flashed like knives. The cavern reverberated with the malevolent shouting, causing the collected filth of ages to rain down on Mire.

"What about those two delectable little boys you told me about?"

"We are still working on it milord," replied Mire, wondering to himself how much longer Stench's patience would hold out.

"What's the holdup this time?"

"Milord, they are well-protected," he said, ducking away from a blow that didn't come. "B-but we are making progress," he offered.

"Give me a full report. Now," Stench bellowed.

"From the beginning?" Mire's voice quaked.

"I need to know where you screwed up," Stench said, closing the distance between him and Mire until they were mere centimeters apart. "We should have had those boys by now," Stench hissed, getting even closer. "The master is not pleased that some human group is still using them in their piddly, little ceremonies."

Mire gripped his crystal as if pulling on the metal chain could help. *Oh no, this is going to be difficult,* he thought, shaking in terror. "It's going to be a long story milord," he said, his knees knocking. "Our Enemy sought to protect those boys from even before they were conceived."

"So? What else is new?" Stench's voice dripped with sarcasm. "Start talking!"

"ELIZABETH, IT'S TIME," floated the voice of Jamie, the wedding coordinator, as I waited in the brides' room. Excited I took one more look in the large mirror; Veil—good; Hair *(I'm glad I grew my hair out)*—good; make-up—good; gown and shoes—great *(I love this dress)*!

The tall, slender green-eyed brunette looking back at me was a true bride.

"Okay, let's go," I said to myself, leaving behind a hurricane aftermath of clothes, make-up, hairdryers, and curling irons. They were abandoned by my bridesmaids and me as we beautified. *Now, if only I could get rid of the negative thoughts* scampering through my mind. The idea that I shouldn't marry the love of my life was ridiculous. *What could possibly be wrong?* My bridesmaids giggling at the entrance to the chapel were waiting. They were excited and happy like I should have been.

My sister, Lily, serving as maid of honor, stuck her head in the stairwell, calling up to me. "Hey, smile!" she said. "You look beautiful!"

So I did. I smiled. It was as bright as I could make it, but my teeth dried out and my cheeks hurt after a bit.

Inside, my nervous brain roiled. *How could marrying him be wrong? He was a strong Christian, intelligent, tall, and good-looking.* I was impressed that he knew a lot about the Old Testament. *Besides,* I thought as I walked, *250 people were sitting in the chapel waiting for me. And Mom and Daddy have already paid for the reception.*

As I reached the bottom of the stairs, I saw Daddy waiting to walk me down the aisle. The bright sunny August afternoon spilled peaceful sunlight through the entrance doors. *Daddy looked so handsome in his tuxedo.* As I slipped my hand into the warm crook of his arm, the bridesmaids made their way down the aisle to the front of the church. I looked down the aisle delighted by the intense colors of the stained-glass windows in the front of the church. My wedding day was as magical as I could have hoped for. Greg waited for me.

I just had cold feet.

I pushed my doubts aside, took a deep breath and stepped forward for the ceremony that would irrevocably change my life.

MIRE DID INDEED start at the beginning of the story so much that Stench soon became bored.

"Okay, okay, you helped that woman chase him and convinced him to marry her. What about the boys?" growled Stench. "She's been taking them to church and singing those awful Christian songs to them. Why didn't you stop her?"

Mire was beginning to realize Stench wasn't going to be satisfied no matter what he told him.

"I did try to stop her. I convinced her husband that church was unnecessary and he quit going. She's such a wimp I thought she'd stop going when he did. Our Enemy gave her unexpected strength."

I WAS SO irritated; I could hardly think.

Sitting in the cramped anteroom at the therapist's office I checked my watch for at least the fifteenth time. The well-used furniture had a peculiar smell, and I had been sitting with it for almost half an hour. I arrived five minutes early as requested. I came prepared to show my underbelly, emotionally. Now twenty minutes later the psychologist had yet to appear. *This is ridiculous,* I thought. *I'm leaving.*

As if on cue the inner office door opened and a short, pudgy, mostly bald man with glasses stood, looking bored. His well-worn brown sweater barely came together over his stomach.

"Mrs. Phillips? Please come in and take a seat," he said. "I'm Dr. Windler."

No apology for keeping me waiting, I thought. I walked into his office and sat down, so annoyed I hardly recognized his décor.

"Now, I need to get some information for your chart," he said as he sat across from me with a clipboard. He pushed his glasses up on the bridge of his nose. "How old are you?"

"Thirty-four"

"Marital status?"

"Married sort of"

"Married, how long?"

"Seven years."

"Any children?"

"Oh, yes, two sons Jonathon and Nicholas," I said with enthusiasm. I began to look around. A bookshelf in need of dusting held many scholarly-looking books. His furniture was old–not antiques, just old. And ugly. I thought I could feel a spring coming up through the seat of my chair.

"Tell me about your sons."

"Jonathon is almost three years old. He is tall for his age with blond hair and blue eyes. And he has the cutest dimples. He is very bright and has an impressive vocabulary. His brother Nicholas is eighteen months old and still has his baby curls." I smiled at the thought of his big expressive brown eyes. "He has freckles on his nose and is proving to be a strong-willed child. But he isn't speaking yet."

Dr. Windler didn't look up from the clipboard. "What brings you into the office today?"

"I don't want to get divorced but I am struggling in my marriage. I asked my husband to come, but he told me 'if you would just straighten up everything would be fine.'" I looked down at my hands in my lap. They were clenched together so I relaxed them. After all, this wasn't the dentist.

"Tell me about your relationship with your husband," he asked in a mechanical voice. I was beginning to wish I had chosen a female therapist.

"Greg is tall, intelligent, handsome," I paused "and self-centered. He has blue eyes and blond hair, which is where the kids get it from. Our relationship was good at first, but lately, our marriage is getting worse and worse. He is gone a lot. Many nights he goes out after work with his friends. He comes home very late smelling of stale cigarette smoke and alcohol." My heart hurt to open up like this. I tried to think of something good. "When he wants to have sex, he can be cordial to me," I said, considering. "But the rest of the time he is inconsiderate, rude, and acts like I'm stupid."

"How is your sex life?"

This guy was starting to get on my nerves.

"His inability to climax during sex was, of course, my fault," I said. We kept at it until he was satisfied or exhausted. I tried everything I knew, but was unable to please him, and he usually laughed at my efforts. I am sore and in pain after sex with him every time." Thinking about it was almost as physically painful as the memory. "I used to wonder what was wrong with women who stayed with abusive men. Now I understand. I am terrified of his anger or disapproval. Even the thought of confronting him about anything makes me almost paralyzed with fear and a little sick to my stomach."

The wrinkles in Dr. Windler's forehead deepened, extending themselves far up his almost bald head. He was quiet, making notes in my chart. I glanced around and watched dust motes dancing in a shaft of sunlight. *Even the windows are dirty.*

"Okay, that's all for today," Dr. Windler said. "Same time next week?"

"Oh, ah, okay," I said, feeling disappointed that Dr. Windler didn't have any suggestions for me. He seemed to be counting the minutes the whole time.

The following week I started my second session with Dr. Windler already irritated. He was late again, and there wasn't a patient ahead of me. "Dr. Windler…" I started to say, but he interrupted me to ask how I was doing. "I'm okay. Nothing has changed since last week."

"What do you want to work on today?"

"I came to therapy because I know God hates divorce, but I can't continue to live like this."

At the mention of God, Dr. Windler frowned slightly and wrinkled his forehead. He made notes on my chart. *I wonder what he is writing; I haven't said anything yet.* I glanced out the window. Today was grey and a little rainy. No dust motes dancing.

"God told me not to marry my husband."

"What?"

Wishing he would pay attention, I said it again.

Dr. Windler looked at me, set down his pen, and put his fingertips together. "How did He do that?"

He wasn't asking for information. He was incredulous that I would believe that.

"Well, it was as if thoughts that weren't mine kept running through my head. Whenever the quiet voice in my head told me there was something amiss, I rationalized. I made excuses in my mind for Greg's unpleasant behavior. I saw our relationship as a good one most of the time. I could not have been more wrong."

"Did you think his unpleasant behavior would improve after

marriage," Dr. Windler asked as he polished his glasses for the umpteenth time.

"I guess I did think that," I confessed.

Dr. Windler said, his condescension heavy like cream on a cloth, "Oh, I see." Evidently, the idea of God caring about and intervening in the lives of His creatures didn't fit his world view.

I was embarrassed by his attitude. My mouth became so dry speaking became difficult. He seemed to revel in my discomfiture. He knew I was uncomfortable, and that appeared to be somehow satisfying for him. I tried unsuccessfully to get my shoulders to relax.

"My husband didn't seem to bond with our sons," I said. "It puzzled me because they were both easy, happy babies. I did notice his behavior toward me seemed to become more abusive after Jonathon, our firstborn, arrived."

"What do you plan to do about this?" Dr. Windler asked distractedly. He seemed bored.

"I don't know; that's why I came to therapy." I felt frustrated and intimidated at the same time. *I am paying for this. What did he want me to say?*

"Ok, time is up for today. Same time next week?" he asked.

I surprised myself by saying, "No, I don't think so."

I thought to myself, *well, at least that was a victory.*

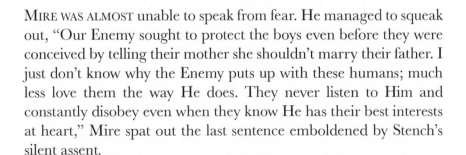

MIRE WAS ALMOST unable to speak from fear. He managed to squeak out, "Our Enemy sought to protect the boys even before they were conceived by telling their mother she shouldn't marry their father. I just don't know why the Enemy puts up with these humans; much less love them the way He does. They never listen to Him and constantly disobey even when they know He has their best interests at heart," Mire spat out the last sentence emboldened by Stench's silent assent.

"The mother is such a pathetic weakling," Stench sneered. Mire nodded, happy to be out of the line of fire. But then Stench turned on Mire and shot "But she's the one who went through with the marriage. That was *her* doing. You had nothing to do with it."

"Y-yeah, but I did get her husband interested in pornography," Mire shot back, terrified. "It led to more dissatisfaction with his wife, which led to strip joints and drinking." Stench stared at Mire, who began trembling again. "The husband's behavior trapped him because he refused help to give it up, and the great part is that he still felt guilty about his behavior. That fabulous tension inside him led him to abuse his weakling of a wife, leave their church friends behind, and eventually get involved with other women in 'one-night stands'. His ruination was glorious, but the very best of all was that he started taking his baby boys with him to his new friends so they could have fun with them."

Mire almost giggled at the thoughts of the terrifying sexual activities to which the two boys were introduced at the perfect ages of eighteen and 36 months.

AFTER READING "LOVE Must Be Tough" by Dr. James Dobson. I realized that my husband had lost respect for me. *Perhaps a trial separation would wake Greg up to what he was doing to our marriage. But how could I possibly tell him?*

At dinner, on one of the nights he came home for dinner, I said, "We need to talk." My stomach was in an uproar. I was so afraid.

"Talk about what," he said in an unpleasant tone.

I struggled to gather up my courage as he looked at me with disdain, and I said, "The boys and I are moving to an apartment. I can't afford the house payment while working part-time so you can stay here." My knees felt like jelly.

"I told you to go back to work full-time, and you wouldn't do it." His fists clenched. I wondered if he was going to hit me. *Surely not in front of the boys!* He stomped out and slammed the front door so hard it rattled the pictures on that wall. *No mention of my leaving him or our marriage failing. Maybe this is what he wants.*

The sharp noises, voices, and emotional tension upset the boys. They both started to cry. I comforted them, promising to read one of their favorite books after bath time. It was clear to me that my defective relationship with Greg was beginning to affect them negatively.

I prayed a lot in the days that followed, but I felt so guilty about making this choice. I needed a sign from the Lord that what I was considering was all right. The moving date was set within a few days of my telling Greg. I couldn't possibly make the move by myself. I decided I would tell my Bible study and work friends and ask for their assistance with the packing and moving. If no one showed up to help, that would be my sign that God was saying "No."

The fateful Saturday for moving dawned. The clear skies promised a beautiful day. I wondered if I would have any help. Looking out the big picture window in the living room, I didn't see anyone or hear a sound. Greg left earlier to go to the gym.

The sound of engines made me look towards the corner. I saw lots of vehicles arriving. *My friends are coming to help, thank you, Lord!* I counted the caravan arriving in front of the house–four trucks and nine adults! What a blessing! I felt a huge weight had lifted off my shoulders.

One of the moms from Bible study took Jon and Nick with her kids to the park for a while. She told me they were going to have McDonald's for lunch– a real treat for them.

We accomplished the move in one trip. With so many hands, the whole move took an hour and a half in spite of stairs in the old house and stairs up to the second-floor apartment. *I really didn't want Greg to come home from his work-out at the gym while we were in the process of moving.*

After dropping off the boys, Liza took me aside to say a private goodbye. "This is for you and the boys," Liza said as she handed me a small envelope.

Inside were coupons for pizza and money to pay for it. That took care of our dinner. I hugged her, squeezing tight because I was so grateful. God not only provided a fun day for my sons, lots of help moving, but also dinner for a tired mom and two excited children.

"SOME SMALL RESISTANCE," Stench said, dismissing the information. "What did you do about it?"

Mire quaked in fear. "I started a fear campaign on the mother with a great nightmare."

Stench looked skeptical.

THE OPENING BELL to start the battle was a dream, a nightmare actually. The most desperate and horrifying period of my life was beginning. It wasn't apparent to me until much later, but this also began a glorious time of seeing God do amazing things in our lives.

The indistinct large shape of a man stood in the doorway to my bedroom, filling the doorway. His shape was not familiar, and I didn't feel safe. There was something evil in his presence. He lumbered into the room, carrying something that appeared heavy. I lay in bed, dressed for sleep and vulnerable. My heart was pounding. Something was very wrong here. He just stood there with something pink in his arms.

It only took a moment for me to see it was a pink plastic laundry basket. He set the basket down in my room. When I saw what was in it, I screamed, "Oh my gosh!"

The basket wasn't really pink. It was white before the blood. I stared frozen in terror and grief as I saw my boys' heads in the basket. Their faces were peaceful—like they were sleeping. No one can live without a head. They were dead! No, not possible. I tried to scream again, but this time, no sound came out. I sobbed as I ran across the hall to their bedroom. My terror was realized as I saw a very small, headless, bloodless body in each crib. My headless babies were still in their blanket sleepers. I tried to scream a third time, but there was only silence. I turned to run out of the boys' room to get some help and tripped over the laundry basket, which had magically been moved. Terrified I tried to scream again when I saw that my head was now in the basket along with the boys'.

I woke up disoriented, shaking and sweating. My heart continued to pound, and I felt like I couldn't breathe. No, this was not possible. I flew out of my bed to check on my sons.

To my unspeakable relief, my little loves were sleeping in their cribs at peace in perfect health. My knees felt weak. I slid down the wall just outside their room, sat on the floor, and sobbed.

Where could this nightmare possibly have come from? I never liked horror movies. Since my separation from Greg, I hadn't been watching anything except Sesame Street and Mister Rogers. I didn't want the boys to see anything scary or violent on the television since they were so young.

I didn't like thinking such horrible things were in my mind. The non-specific terror associated with the dream did not fade but clung to my mind like a cold, wet cloak. I just couldn't shake it off. There wasn't anyone I could talk to about the nightmare. It was too horrible to impose on a loved one and I had fired my therapist after his uncaring attitude became too much to bear.

After a time, I was finally able to relegate the memory to a place where it wasn't constantly on my mind. Through the press of everyday life, taking care of the boys, working, and being with friends, I came back to myself. Eventually, the memory and associated apprehension faded a bit. But if I happened to think of it, the dream was as vivid, as terrifying, and as horrible as it had been that awful night.

"OKAY, OKAY," STENCH admitted the nightmare was adequate for a start. "Is that all?"

"I sent several minor harassing spirits to whisper in her ear."

"Whisper what?"

Mire's courage picked up a bit. "Oh, lots of different things like 'you've been really apathetic toward your God' or 'what makes you think He is going to listen to you much less help you?' Oh, and 'You are a lousy wife. It's your fault your husband used pornography, went to strip joints, and had affairs' I think the most successful lines were 'You have done irreparable psychological damage to your sons. They'll never be all right. Their father is going to kidnap them, and you'll never see them again. You lost your temper and yelled the other day. You are a rotten mother.' Mire was confident in his list of horrible thought-darts. He knew they'd hit their mark.

Stench seemed somewhat interested now.

I DID NOT want to get divorced.

I know God hates it, and I took my vows very seriously. However, I was under increasing emotional strain and my supervisor told me it was starting to affect my work performance. That was embarrassing. I was not accustomed to anything but glowing reports from supervisors.

It upset Nick and Jon when they would occasionally catch me crying. I read the Scriptures about divorce and God's hatred for it, but I also heard several respected Christian speakers, as well as my own pastor, talk about how God loves us and doesn't want us abused.

The thoughts in my mind went back and forth like the ball in a tennis match; *divorce, reconciliation, legal separation, mediation?* I was so agitated I could hardly pray anymore. I began to feel like an unpeeled potato cooking in a microwave, about to explode! *Would I be forced to initiate the divorce?* I felt restless and uneasy in a way I couldn't explain to anyone. *Was there truly something sinister and evil going on, or was it just my imagination?*

I found myself checking the only door to the apartment to be sure it was locked several times during each evening. The only thing that kept my fear from becoming outwardly evident was my desire not to frighten Jon and Nick. *Am I just being paranoid? Besides, come on, realistically, what could possibly be wrong?*

On Jon's third birthday three weeks after our move I put on a birthday party for him. I invited my Bible study friends and their children. I asked Greg, Greg's dad and his new wife, and Greg's mom and her new husband to join us as well. My little apartment was bursting at the seams; lots of joy and laughter. I wasn't sure what to expect from Greg and his family. I had some trepidation because I hadn't seen or spoken to him since the separation. Everyone except Greg's dad, who was creepy as usual, was cordial. And I'll never forget the sight of six little kids kicking balloons around the living room and giggling. I tried to make things as fun as possible for Jon. My brother and sister-in-law, Uncle Jim and Aunt Brenda, brought a great cake with Jon's favorite dinosaur on it. They were helpful with crowd control, and I was so grateful for their generosity.

It didn't occur to me until later that Greg had very little inter-action with either Jon or Nick with one exception. There were lots of gifts, but Greg insisted that Jon play with the toy he brought to the exclusion of any others. *That was weird. After all, who is the adult here?*

The next morning, I opened the door to Maria, our nanny. "Good morning," we both said. We smiled at our simultaneous salutation.

"Hey, Guys!" I called out. Maria is here, and I'm leaving for work!" I wished I didn't have to leave them to go to work even part-time. I trusted Maria implicitly, but I just couldn't shake the intangible uneasiness I felt. The feeling was real but elusive when

I tried to pin it down in my mind. And the cause of this uncomfortable feeling escaped me.

There was just a sense of evil around and I–

"My turn Mommy!" Jon said arriving at a run from their bedroom looking for a hug.

"Okay, and tomorrow will be Nick's turn to be first for hugs." Nick nodded vigorously.

"Thanks, Maria, I'll see you all this evening. Nick and Jon, be good for Maria. I love you both very much!"

During my commute, I tried to figure out why I had these ominous feelings of doom. Leaving Greg and the house we shared, gave me much needed relief from the oppression I felt. I felt a lurking sense of evil I couldn't get rid of. As I tried to figure it out, I realized that there was a great deal of oppression at the house we had lived in with Greg. I guess it's one of those things you don't realize is happening because you are so accustomed to it. Getting out from under the bad feelings brought much-needed relief, but my intuition that something was wrong was still very strong.

I thought of the Christmas we shared right before I separated from the boys' father. Jon, Nick, and I went to Jim and Brenda's home overnight. My mom and dad were visiting from out of state, but Greg didn't go with us. Even though he had always gotten along well with Jim and Brenda, and it was a family holiday time, he just didn't seem to want to be a part.

Both Nick and Jon kept telling me how much fun they were having, although we did very little except sit around and talk. I had a wonderful time myself. It wasn't until much later that I realized why we had such a good time and why it was so hard to return home.

Nick and Jon clouded up and started to cry when I said we needed to get ready to go home. They wanted all of us to stay with Aunt Brenda and Uncle Jim permanently.

Now that we moved out there was a greater sense of lightness and clarity. The boys smiled more. But there was still something amiss. I knew things were better now that we were away from Greg and the house we lived in together. But I was so wrong to think everything was anywhere close to okay.

CHAPTER 2

THEY ALL WALKED out the door, Nick looking back at me with an expression on his face that tore my heart. A few moments later, I stood alone in the house, lost since my boys were gone for the weekend. I looked around trying to figure out something to do to occupy myself when there was a knock on the door. My ex-husband was standing there alone. Panicked and angry, I said, "Where are the boys?"

He looked disgusted and said, "They're in my car. I need a jump; my battery is dead."

"You left them in the car alone?" I said with incredulity.

"Sure, why not?" He answered flippantly. I stared at him a moment. His behavior shouldn't have shocked me at this point, but it always seemed to. I shook my head and said, "Let me get my keys."

I drove my car around the building to where he told me he was parked. Both Nick and Jon were crying strapped in their car seats when I got there. I couldn't believe he left them alone in the car in the parking lot.

While their dad used the jumper cables, I went to see why they were crying. I leaned into the backseat of his two-door car and both boys put their arms out. They were trying to get out of their car seats to get to me. As I tried to comfort them and figure out what was wrong, Greg grabbed my arm and pulled me away.

"You're making them upset," he accused.

I was so shocked I didn't know what to say. I stood there so put off I didn't even realize that his car was running, and Greg unhooked the jumper cables from his battery. He went around to the driver's side, got in, told the boys to *shut up*, and sped away. I was left standing in the parking lot—jumper cables still attached to my battery and dangling from the front of my car. I was devastated by Jon's and Nick's pleas to get out and I couldn't help but be afraid I'd never see them again.

I had been counting the hours until their return. *There was a part of me that always worried he wouldn't bring them back.* Thank God it wasn't long before there was a knock on the door and Greg stepped inside. Nick and Jon ran around their dad to come to me, each grabbing tight on to my legs. I was so glad to see them; I could hardly speak.

Greg stood at the door and said, "Good-bye guys. See you in a couple of weeks." Neither boy responded. A little more loudly Greg called out, "I'm trying to tell you guys good-bye!"

Greg was becoming angry. This wasn't out of the norm, but I didn't want to disturb our neighbors. "Jon and Nick," I said, "please go give your dad a hug good-bye." With reluctance, the boys complied, but returned immediately to me. Greg was cavalier with his embrace, and as soon as they were back with me, he stomped out, slamming the door.

Both boys seemed very quiet while I got them ready for bed. I noticed a peculiar smell when I got their hair wet to wash it in the bath. I didn't recognize the odor. Something like old cigarette smoke, and alcohol from a bar, but there was also something exotic smelling. *Where in the world have they been?* I wondered. *Where did Greg take them?*

"Did you guys have fun at your dad's?" They did not respond. "What did you all do?" Both boys continued playing very studiously with their toys. As we finished up their baths, I wrapped each one in a fluffy towel. I almost chuckled to myself because they were still so small the bath towels seemed to engulf them.

"Let's go get jammies on," I said brightly. "Shall we race to the bedroom tonight?"

This seemed to pull them back to life. They took off towards their bedroom, and I had to laugh as both boys dropped their towels so they could run faster.

When we were done cheering and laughing, we chose their pj's and the bedtime story. The boys became serious once again.

"I..is... D...da...ad gone?" Jon asked.

Why is he stuttering? I wondered. "Yes, Honey, he went home. You saw him leave, remember? Did you need something from him?"

"N…n...NO!" Jon said. Although stuttering badly, he still nearly shouted.

"Okay, just checking.

Jon twitched a little. "M...My...My b...b…bottom hurts," he said. *What? What could have happened?* My heart began to pound, and my stomach clenched.

"Where does it hurt? Can you show me where it hurts the most?"

He pointed toward his rectal area. My heart sank. *Elizabeth,* I thought to myself, *don't jump to conclusions. Maybe he had a hard stool or something.*

"Did you fall or something?" I asked, hoping my worst fears were imagined.

"N...no, it just hurts."

Fear gripped my mind.

"Well let's get your diaper and jammies on," I said, making myself sound calm. Here, let's put on some ointment. Maybe that will make it feel better."

As I applied the ointment, I tried to see if there was any sign of…I don't know what. My mind raced even though I couldn't see anything amiss. From all I could see his little bottom and rectal area looked normal. He didn't mention it after I put the ointment in the area.

Crisis averted, I hoped. Finishing our nighttime routine of songs and prayers, we snuggled in our bentwood and wicker rocking chair. I had one boy on each knee, and we giggled together, reading our bedtime stories. My arms around both of them I said, "Do you guys know that this is the favorite part of my day?"

"We know that m…m…Mommy. That's what you always s…s… say," Jon replied.

"Honey, you sound a little sad. Is everything OK?"

Neither of my boys responded. They just looked at each other with fear and sorrow in their eyes.

"D…d…Do we have to go to d…d…Dad's again?" Jon asked in quieter tones.

"Well, he wants you to visit in two weeks for the weekend. Is that okay?"

Again, the knowing glances but no verbal response.

"We'll pack your favorite blankets and toys. I bet you'll have a good time. Tell you what, I'll even get you a special treat from the store for you to take along." There wasn't even a smile at the prospect of a new toy. Seeing their fear-filled faces I wondered where this was all coming from. "You guys know you can tell me anything, right?" They simply looked at each other and didn't meet my eyes.

I put them each in their own crib with a hug and a kiss. After their bath, Jon and Nick now smelled of baby shampoo—nothing like that weird smell from before.

"I love you both lots! Sleep tight"

I paused momentarily in the hall outside their room putting my hand on the door jamb to say a silent prayer for them.

The stuttering is a different story. Why would he suddenly begin stuttering? I thought even as I prayed.

The next day I called my mom, who is a pediatric RN (Registered Nurse) to ask what she thought about Jon's new affliction. She thought it was odd since Jon had been speaking clearly and in complete sentences since he was twelve months old. She told me three-year-old's do stutter occasionally and perhaps a call to their doctor wouldn't hurt. I called Dr. Pete, our pediatrician, who happened to be Jonathon's godfather.

"Hi, Pete, sorry to bother you," I said when he answered the phone. I explained my concerns and questioned the need for a visit. "We can come in to see you if you think it is necessary."

Pete was not unduly concerned either. Since I felt a good relationship with their father was important to their development, I tried to set my qualms aside. *Besides,* I thought, *what choice did I have? I knew Greg interacted with them better if they were happy and cooperative. I'll try to 'psyche them up' before they go next time.*

As the days passed, I noticed Jonathon was spending an increasing amount of time squished as far back in the corner of the cushions of our overstuffed sofa as he could go. His face was solemn, and he was always holding his Megan (a small stuffed dog) and his quilt. He looked so sad it broke my heart. I felt like crying myself. He was obviously hurting, and I couldn't fix it.

"Jon, can you tell Mommy what's wrong?"

"I'm j...just s...s...sad."

Nick heard Jon say he was sad and went into their room. He returned with a bucket of Lego bricks. Jon just shook his head.

"I'll play Legos with you, Nick," I said, hoping Jon would get interested and join us. He still refused.

Nick and I each raced to finish our buildings. I imitated a small crash, and we joyfully knocked them down. I think that was the most fun for Nick. Jon stared off into space; no interest at all. After we cleaned up the Legos, I turned back to Jon asking, "Jon do you want to read a book?"

"N...no...no, M...mo...mommy," he replied. His voice was soft, just above a whisper

"How about a game?" I tried again.

He turned his face to the wall. I checked his forehead for fever and even though I didn't detect a fever decided to call Dr. Pete again.

After quick pleasantries and a brief explanation Dr. Pete sighed.

"Well Elizabeth I think it would be a good idea to have Jon evaluated by a child psychiatrist. How long have his current symptoms been going on?" Dr. Pete asked.

"At least three weeks," I replied.

"OK here's the name and number of someone I recommend. Please let me know how it goes."

Our first session with the psychiatrist Dr. Zadoff was less than stellar. He wouldn't let Nick in the exam room and Jon refused to talk to him. We had several more weekly sessions with Dr. Zadoff with little progress. Jon never opened up to him about anything of significance, but Jon would answer direct questions from the doctor with one or two-word answers. Dr. Zadoff's only suggestion was that Jon had self-esteem issues and no real recommendations for treatment except for more time with his father. I mentioned the stuttering and reluctance to visit his dad, but the psychiatrist pooh-poohed that as not indicating anything. My mom-heart was suspicious, concerned, and hurting but no one I had talked to seemed to share my concerns.

Several months after Jon's birthday party I hosted one for Nick's second birthday. My mom and dad were visiting, and Nick and Jon were so happy to see their grandparents.

"Wh…wh…what's that Grandpa?" Jon asked.

"That's a video camera. Want me to take your picture?" Grandpa said with a smile.

"Yeah. D…d…do we have to take our clothes off?" Jon asked. His innocent question brought a shocking chill to my body.

"No that's not necessary," my dad said with a slightly strangled voice. He tried to smile but there was no hiding his astonishment. My Dad looked at me, a question in his eyes. I just lifted my shoulders in a silent question.

"This is recording moving pictures so you can jump around if you like."

Both boys proceeded to jump around and be silly. Then Grandpa showed them the tape he had recorded. Nick and Jon were excited to see themselves on the tiny camera screen.

"I thought I would record your birthday party, Nick, then you and Jon and your mom can watch it anytime you like. Want to?"

Jon and Nick looked hard at each other. "M...m...Mommy will D...d...Dad be here?" Jon asked.

Puzzled, I said "I think so. I invited him, your other grand-parents, and the Bible study kids." The boys' smiles faded.

After the guests had departed and the boys went to Greg's for the weekend, we viewed the birthday party tape recording. My parents and I were struck by the expressions on Nick's face. He never smiled throughout the entire party games, gifts, goodies, and cake—nothing elicited a real smile. Even when he was acting silly, it never brought a genuinely happy expression from his face. The more I watched the more I realized there was *no* smile at all. Nick was still not speaking yet just making his wishes known by gestures and other charades sometimes with humorous results or looking to Jon to 'translate.'

A couple of weeks later on Thursday the phone rang. "Hello," I answered.

The unwelcome tones of my ex-husband's voice came over the phone.

"Hi, I won't be able to pick the boys up until Saturday this weekend. You didn't have anything planned on Friday night, right? I mean," he said chuckling, "you never do. But I have a party to go to," he finished.

"They might be disappointed you know." I stuffed my feelings down trying to remain cordial.

"Oh, they'll get over it. And, oh yeah, the child support is going to be late again." *As usual, no apology, no reason. I just have to accept it, I guess.*

"Okay, what time do you want me to have them ready on Saturday?"

"I'll pick them up at 2:30 in the afternoon. You'll have them ready right?"

"Yes, they'll be ready." I promptly hung up the phone. I thought it rude, but I also felt a little pleasure at doing it.

This scheduling conversation was becoming frequent lately. I can't say I minded though. I still wasn't sure why Nick and Jon's behavior was so different when they thought they were going on a visit with Greg. They became erratic, whiny, teary, and clingy whenever there was a visit looming. Tonight, as in the past, hearing that their dad wouldn't be picking them up on Friday they relaxed. As if a warning light was turned off their behavior shifted back to normal.

That night the shift in their attitude and behavior was brought to my attention when Jon said hopefully," D…d…does this mean we don't have to go to D…Dad's?'"

"He'll be here to get you tomorrow afternoon," I said and watched his little face break into a million pieces of sadness and fear.

As I sipped my tea after the boys cried themselves to sleep the deep ache in my heart continued. I thought about what to do when Greg picked them up tomorrow.

Do I dare confront him? Is that even a wise thing to do? I was trying very hard to trust God. All I could see was the pain and emotional disruption in my little boys' lives. *Was it just the separation and divorce? Was there another more sinister reason?*

STENCH LOOKED AT Mire out of the corners of his eyes and said "I don't think your campaign is going so well. She seems to be getting stronger not weaker."

Mire grabbed his crystal again and said "How was I to know she would put her sons' needs before her own? I did get their dad to bring them to the ceremonies so his friends could terrify them into urinating and defecating." Mire noticed Stench's mouth seemed to begin watering a bit at that thought.

"Ah the power produced by the fluids of the innocents mixed in with the sacrificial drink," Stench said as he fairly groaned with desire." There is nothing that gives more strength and power except of course sacrifice itself."

CHRISTMASTIME AGAIN; ONE of our favorite times of the year. This year Jon was three and a half and Nick slightly over two. I was anxious and concerned this particular year because it was Greg's turn to have the boys. They would be at his apartment for Christmas Day and the following week. *It would be such a long time, especially since it seemed something weird was going on.*

My mom and dad were visiting from Montana that year and we attended Christmas Eve services together with the boys. I took the boys over to Greg's apartment after the service feeling the urge not to go, to just turn the car around and face the consequences of keeping the boys with me. I kept driving and found myself in his parking lot still wondering. As soon as I unbuckled the car seats. Jon and Nick both started crying not wanting to get out of the car at all. Jon was trying to re-buckle his car seat. So we could leave.

"M…M…Mommy this is Dad's house. Please don't leave us here."

My heart was about to burst with sorrow. *What can I do?* I had to verbally force them out of the car sternly insisting. —Doing it felt like pushing a knife in my heart. Jon and Nick appeared resigned to their fate as we walked up the sidewalk to Greg's apartment. Greg got angry when he saw that they had been crying and I left quickly to hide my own tears.

Later in the week I called Greg. "Mom and Daddy are leaving mid-week. They live so far away and were hoping to see the boys once more to take them to lunch. May we?" "I requested.

"No," he said without any hesitation. "This is my week. You're already getting them back on New Year's Eve instead of New Year's Day."

"That was the arrangement you made because you have parties to go to remember?"

"Well, okay." he said conceding "But this is it!"

"All right, we'll pick them up at 11:30 tomorrow. Thank you." When we arrived, Nick was asleep on the sofa. *He needs a diaper change* I thought *but I'll do it in the car.* As I woke him he initially looked terrified and tried to squirm away. Realizing it was me Nick threw his arms around my neck and wouldn't let go even to get his jacket on. Jon already had on his jacket and was pushing and scrambling trying to get Grandma and himself out the door as quickly as possible. I was shocked and stricken by the grey pallor of their skin and the deadness of their eyes. My parents' surprised quizzical expressions indicated that they noticed as well.

Good. It wasn't just my imagination.

As our meal at their favorite restaurant progressed the light returned to their eyes and they became their usual animated selves. They both wanted to be in physical proximity with me every minute which I found odd. We laughed and talked a lot though, with Nick making gestures.

And then the time came for them to return to their dad's apartment for the remaining three days of the visit.

As I pulled the car into the parking lot for Greg's apartment complex, Jon recognized it. He said "M…m… Mommy, no! This is dad's apartment. What are we doing here?" His voice got higher as he figured out that they were returning to their dad's place.

Nick started to cry and shook his head vigorously. Jon started to cry too. They were devastated that they were not going home with me.

PANIC! My brain was reeling. Trying hard not to cry myself "Guys, I don't have any choice here. The courts have said that you need to spend this time with your dad.

I have never ever wanted to do anything less than I wanted to walk my two small sons up the sidewalk to their dad's apartment. Once again, I felt a weight of shame slam into my spine as I prepared to hand over my babies——*to what fate?* My parents waited in the car while I dragged my feet up the walk. *I felt like my heart was being squeezed in a vise. There was something desperately wrong here and I couldn't figure it out or protect my little boys.* My mind raced as I racked my brain for a reason, they should go with me. *My brain won't work–I'm too upset to think clearly.*

I rang the doorbell. *Please don't be home. Please, please don't be home.* There was a brief second of hope as he didn't answer the door right away. But then I heard his footsteps inside the apartment coming toward the door—ominous and inevitable. My heart was in my boots. I was going to have to leave them. *Oh God, please no.* Both boys started crying again. When Greg opened the door and found them crying and clinging to me, he got angry. Strangely despite his evident emotion Greg's blue eyes were dead-looking—like a shark's.

"What did you and your parents do to upset them?" he asked with rage shaking in his voice.

Incredulous at his accusation I opened my mouth to reply but couldn't speak. I wanted to ask him why they were so reluctant to stay with him, but I was afraid he might take it out on them. I knelt in the snow and hugged each one in turn, told them I loved them and would see them in a few days. I looked up at Greg, pleading with my eyes to cut the visit short, but his angry, dead eyes denied my request. He grabbed an arm on each boy and yanked them into the apartment slamming his door in my face. I heard the lock click into place and stood up, looking at the closed door for a moment. And then I turned away weeping all the way back to the car. My parents and I were devastated, and we didn't know what to do. They had to fly home that day.

What can I do? I am frantic Lord! Please help me know what to do! What can I do to protect my children? Ideas ran around in my mind like greyhounds on a track. One by one, I rejected every idea I could come up with. From what I read I knew the courts would not listen to my 'mom-heart' concerns; especially unsubstantiated beliefs about any possible abusive activity. I feared the court would side with my nice-looking, intelligent, normal-acting ex-husband with his 'wide-eyed' denial of any problems with the visitation. Then it would be assumed I was just a bitter vindictive ex-wife trying to steal his children and poison their hearts and minds against him.

I am so worried the court will increase his visitation, or Heaven forbid, give him custody I can hardly think. I felt caught in a trap. Between the visitation orders of the divorce court and allowing my sons to continue in a situation that caused them fear and possible harm, I fretted until I bit my fingernails bloody. My worries seemed to loom larger and larger like huge crashing waves against my psyche. *What can I do? I feel overwhelmed drowning in uncertainty.* Suddenly, a quiet thought broke through the chaos and I had the sure feeling I was not wholly powerless. *The God of the universe would still hear my prayers.*

I started to pray respectfully as I always did. I tried to be polite but then I felt anger like an avalanche overtake me. And I couldn't lie to myself or to God. Even in prayer.

I was furious.

"Why haven't You protected them?! I pray every day, but You are allowing Greg to do who knows what and *hurt* them. These are Your children! Don't You care what's happening to them?! How could You let these horrible things I have imagined go on?" Fear, anxiety, and desperation rose in me like a tsunami tide. "How are our lives ever going to be normal again? How can I help the boys when I don't even know what's going on? Why aren't you protecting them?" I almost shouted. I was sure He would strike me down as I sobbed my furious accusations at Him.

God did not strike me down and it was just the beginning of a new prayer life for me. Somehow in my childhood I had received the message that anger was never acceptable, particularly to authority figures, and especially towards God Almighty. I should only go to the Lord with my Sunday-best thoughts and carefully worded prayers, always happy and grateful, obedient, (at least outwardly) and cheerful. My prayers were crafted 'showing' Him the parts of me designed to win the approval of the people around me. *Kinda silly since I know He knows everything about everyone and everything.*

I decided to start being honest about my feelings when I prayed. But I had to admit my lingering concern: He would accept me and love me if I expressed how I really felt, and thought *wouldn't He?*

STENCH NEARLY HOWLED with frustration "She's learning she can trust our Enemy! Now she's appealing to our Foe! Do you know what that means Mire, do you?" Stench yelled his eyes flashing and his ghastly odoriferous breath choking Mire and burning his eyes. Mire nodded slowly realizing his doom was near, because God always responded to honest prayers from His children.

For Mire there was no one to call on and he knew all was lost. Stench wheeled on him, blue-black lightning flashing from his eyes. With an outstretched fingertip Stench sent a shot of his power forth, forcing Mire into the abyss. With the sound of a thunderous crack, Mire was no more, and his small power passed into Stench.

Stench said to himself "That's the end of our difficulties getting those little boys. Mire was hopelessly incompetent. I'll make quick work of this project myself." He stopped in his gloating for a moment trying to decide which approach would be the most efficient. A direct terrorizing attack on that mother would be the most enjoyable but with her renewed relationship with the Enemy she might surprise him.

"No," he thought aloud "I'll send some harassing spirits to remind her she is still under her ex-husband's control. Thanks to the effective job he did with the emotional and sexual abuse that should be easy."

It made Stench laugh when he thought about the generational curses on Greg's family. Greg thought he was so powerful, and it was really just the effect of curses of abuse. They were handed down from father to son without any awareness on their part. That helped the husband with his efforts to abuse his wife. Greg was unaware of the part he was now playing in the master's plan. Stench had heard reports that this malleable human was seeking power, sex, and money through that piddling little local group's activities. He grinned and said, "Those stupid humans have no idea what they are messing with."

He had also heard the group had 'stepped up their game' and sacrificed a runaway teenager. "No one will ever miss that kid," Stench said with a broad smile to no one. The master was only slightly pleased, giving them a tidbit of power to keep them active in his service. Stench laughed again.

Mid-chortle a huge misshapen hand closed around his throat stopping his breath. His eyes bulged as he looked into the face of his superior Filth.

Malevolence filled the room in palpable waves. Filth had an almost human quality to his grotesque face but carried massive black wings that draped about him. Extreme hatred and fear rolled from him, like fog roils off a river. Filth hissed in a sinister whisper "What are you laughing about? We still do not have those boys."

Chapter 3

THE BOYS WERE so happy when they found out they would be home the next weekend. I saw Jon's dimples for the first time in a good long while. Now four years old it was good to see some of the sparkle come back into his eyes. Nick was almost three and loved dressing like a cowboy or a soldier. Today he was a cowboy. It was Friday evening and Jon asked "C…c…Can we watch our S…s…Sesame S…s…Street tape?"

I said "Not right now. I'm using the VCR to record a movie named 'Firefox' off the TV."

"C…c…Can we watch it?" Jon asked.

"We'll see. I want to watch it first and make sure it is OK for you to watch it."

Jon had a peculiar look on his face when he asked "D…d… Does it have guns and people uncovering their b…b…bottoms in it?"

He was four! What would he know about exposed bottoms?

Blown away I did my best to keep a straight face. Due to divine providence I'd recently read several articles about how to conduct yourself when a child reveals information about possible abuse. I had no idea that when I was reading the articles, I would soon need the information for my own children.

The gist of the articles was that it was imperative to be calm and matter of fact about a child's revelations. The authors stressed that the child needed to be affirmed and whatever truth they were trying to impart needed to be accepted at face value.

Jon's knowledge was inappropriate for his age and I didn't teach or allow anything like that anywhere near my toddlers. Where would he learn this material?

I steeled myself and asked Jon, keeping my voice clear of emotion "Have you seen a movie like that?"

He avoided meeting my eyes and said "Yeah. At Dad's."

I seethed with anger when I heard his answer. But I did my best to keep my face calm and pleasant. Several months earlier when I noticed that the boys' father left his pornography magazines out on the coffee table in his apartment, I asked him to put them away while the boys were visiting. His response would later haunt me.

"You have nothing to say about what happens when Jon and Nick are with me," he said. As I recalled the situation, I remembered how his face glowered with anger.

"Have you seen other movies or TV shows like that?" I asked, trying to remain calm and gentle.

Jon responded to my question with a strange dance of avoidance. "I want to tell you about... (casting his eyes around the room) m-my...my...Legos."

Nick became still as stone staring at Jon with round startled eyes. It was apparent that Jon and Nick were on the same wavelength and knew things I was not privy to. I was stricken to the heart by the somber fearful looks they gave each other.

"Okay," I said. "What about your Legos?" I hoped to hear an answer related to something they had built.

Jon responded, "I want to tell you about th-th-the...t-t-table." Neither of my sons would meet my eyes by this point in the conversation. But it was so obvious Jon and Nick were so distressed that I decided not to force them to relive something so upsetting. I changed the subject.

It was time for our bath, prayer and singing routine. We did it each night before bed and I couldn't get to that piece of 'normal' soon enough.

My fear and curiosity were like piranhas chewing up my insides, but we did our bedtime routine giggling, playing, and talking about mundane things. After multiple reassurances that they did not have to go with their dad the next day they drifted off to sleep.

I was in a total uproar inside.

Sitting down in the living room I forced myself to take slow breaths. I was livid! I could feel the blood pounding in my head. I considered calling Greg and confronting him about allowing the boys to see pornography. But a little voice in my head told me to wait, that it was not a good idea). As enraged as I was, I still feared the thought of confronting him. I knew he would be angry with me. My fury and fear might lead to my usual tongue-tied state around him. Then he would mock me for being unable to express what I wanted to say. It was always so easy for him to deflect anything I wanted to get across. For some time, he had known and used all my vulnerabilities against me with great success. He had no respect for me, and it showed in his communications with me. This was not the first time I was 'instructed' by the still small voice in my head. Scared and exhausted I chased sleep until the wee hours of the morning.

Saturday morning came and both Nick and Jon glowed with cheerfulness. They were content to read and color in their coloring books all day. I tried to read a little bit, but I couldn't focus on my novel. Even though our apartment was small the boys insisted on following me from room to room. I felt uneasy about going out of the apartment, so I was happy that the boys and I had a quiet start to our weekend. Jon reiterated several times "I'm s…s…so glad we don't have to go to D…d…Dad's today."

Then Jon said "I don't want to see Matt and Sara today either.

"Who's that?" I asked in a light tone of voice. My senses went on high alert and I saw both boys look at me with a surprised expression. "You know M…m…Mommy." Nick and Jon gave each other a look of deep sadness. I decided not to pursue it.

Sunday afternoon we relaxed after church and made a visit to Nick and Jon's favorite restaurant. My curiosity got the best of me. I knew it wasn't a good idea and might upset the boys but I asked about Matt and Sara.

Jon said with hesitation in his voice "They are friends of D…d… Dad. You know." Nick's big brown eyes were sad but wary. After Jon's comment neither boy would say more. I was scared, furious, and desperate to figure out what was going on.

Everything they said was forming a puzzle with missing pieces for me. Jon mentioned a few weeks ago that their dad had taken pictures of them and given them to Matt. If I had been paying closer attention, I might have noted that Jon's expression while mentioning the pictures was strange. But I didn't catch it—that time. Oblivious, I said "Matt must be a good friend of your dad to want pictures of you." They looked at each other and then at me as if I was crazy.

For both of them their affect changed, like they were closing a door on me. When that happened the alarm bells in my 'Mom heart' were not tinkling, chiming, or ringing. They were now a full-fledged cacophony. I would discover only much later that at this point Jon and Nick were convinced that I knew about and was okay with everything being done to them just as Greg and his associates had been telling them.

I was fortunate to have the next day off, and although I knew Mondays were the busiest day in a pediatrics office, I called Dr. Pete. I trusted him implicitly. He knew my ex-husband quite well though he had not seen him in some time since Greg no longer attended our Bible study. He had a very long day, so it was about 7:30pm before he called me back.

"Elizabeth?" Pete's reassuring voice asked as I picked up the phone "What's up?"

"Hi Pete. Thanks for calling me back. I'm worried about Jon and Nick," I said and started to choke up with tears.

"What about Jon and Nick?" he said, his concern coming through the phone line as he adjusted to my stress level.

"I'm afraid Greg is abusing them or letting someone else abuse them."

"Well that's quite a statement. I haven't seen him in a while, but I think I know him pretty well. What is causing you concern?"

"Jon's sudden onset of stuttering and Nick still isn't speaking much at all even though he's almost three. Jon's stuttering becomes markedly worse when a visit is impending. And both boys are very sad when they have to go to Greg's. They turn into almost completely different children." I must have sounded like I was medicated. I couldn't get the words out fast enough.

"Jon has said many times he doesn't want to go to their dad's house. But the admission that his bottom hurt, though I couldn't see anything, as well as watching pornography…" I explained Jon's mention of 'a movie with people uncovering their bottoms.'

Pete was quiet and I kept going before I forgot anything. "And the things they *aren't* saying. All of it. All of it is making me so suspicious. They even smell funny when they come back from a visit to Greg. Every time…" Tears threatened to overwhelm me again.

"Okay that's a lot going on. I must admit I am concerned. I'd like to see them in the office this week. Is there anything else you want to tell me?" He asked with a calm gentle voice utilizing his good bedside manner.

"When Greg and I were still together, and Jon was about two I think, Greg spanked him so hard that it left a mark on Jon's bottom through a double cloth diaper plastic pants and pajama bottoms. Greg never did it again but now I wish I had told you and taken a picture of the handprint when I saw it during a diaper change. Nick still isn't speaking much, and my friend who is a speech therapist said it was unusual for a child his age not to have more and clearer speech."

Pete was quiet for an uncomfortable length of time. I almost wondered if he were still on the phone. Finally, he spoke "I have a high index of suspicion when it comes to child abuse. But all of the things you have just told me about can very well be indicators of child abuse. I'm sorry to be blunt Elizabeth but I think you should call 'The Center' in the morning and discuss the situation with them."

I don't remember ending the call. When he mentioned The Center my ears began to ring with my panic.

Most people where I lived knew of The Center, a world-renowned organization for the treatment of abused children and adult survivors of childhood abuse. Hearing the name struck me like a bell, and my thoughts went to war.

This is horrible! I don't know what I expected Pete to say, but his suggestion left me feeling unable to breathe. My blood ran cold and my fingers and toes turned to ice cubes. Meanwhile my heart was in a tightening vise. I had been worried about all kinds of bad things going on. To hear the actual word 'abuse' from someone I respected catapulted my very worst fears into reality.

CHAPTER 4

FILTH THREW STENCH down. "Do something with that woman," he said. "Now she plans to call The Center for assistance. We can't have that! How about giving her a big dose of fear?"

I LOOKED AT the red numbers on my digital clock. 1:04 in the morning! *You've got to be kidding.* Only 15 minutes had passed since the last time I looked. *Elizabeth,* I told myself *you've got to stop thinking about this.* I thought *just lie still and close your eyes...*

No dice.

Okay another drink of water. I checked on the boys on my way to the bathroom. They were sleeping peacefully. *Nick's sweet little snore makes me smile. Okay back to bed.* I looked at the clock again. 1:34. I felt like throwing it across the room. *Lie still and relax.*

I couldn't turn my mind off.

Dr. Pete was cautious. He wouldn't have even suggested abuse unless he was sure.

That wretched clock now read 2:32 then 3:47; 4:05; 5:10. *This is ridiculous* I thought. *I might as well get up.*

The Tuesday morning hours dragged by. I somehow kept myself busy until 9:00 am when The Center opened. I was loathed to admit it, but I had been nursing a horrible thought. Along with my rage over something being done to my children, there was a small but increasing feeling I was going to be 'in trouble' with Greg. It actually made me afraid to pursue things.

Such are the scars of the abuse I'd received.

Jon and Nick were playing in their room. I needed to make the call while they were preoccupied.

My fingers shaking, I placed the call to The Center.

"You have reached the intake line for The Center. All counselors are currently assisting other clients. Please do not hang up. A counselor will be with you very shortly."

Wow, I thought, *how sad that there are so many people needing assistance with this kind of issue.*

"Hello. Sorry to keep you waiting. my name is Kathleen, how can I help you?

I explained the situation to Kathleen being very careful not to overstate anything or make accusations beyond what I had evidence for. My reticence to accuse or be hysterical must have been a gift from the Holy Spirit.

The counselor took her time and with great care she responded to my mom-heart.

"I feel there is a real cause for concern here ma'am. But the Center is more of a treatment facility," Kathleen said. "We don't get involved with the legal aspects except when the courts assign someone to receive treatment. This seems to be a dangerous situation. Please call Social Services and request to speak to an intake Social Worker.

"Thank you, Kathleen I appreciate your time."

"Best of luck to you and your sons."

A legal issue? *Why hadn't it occurred to me that child abuse is a crime?* I wanted to protect and care for my children. I was naïve to think my children could be protected without legal intervention. I was frightened of confronting my ex-husband. I had no idea what he would do when he found out I had called the authorities, but I knew he would be furious. I worried that he might take it out on the boys to punish me.

I decided not to call Social Services until the boys took their afternoon nap, so they didn't hear me on the phone. The waiting was painful. A part of me knew I had to call but I felt very shaky. I spoke to several people before being transferred to a woman who put me at ease as soon as she heard the tone of my voice.

I told her what I'd told Dr. Pete and shared The Center's recommendation that I call Social Services. She was very calm but insistent on seeing the boys as soon as possible. She was working a later shift with several appointments already booked but asked if I could bring Jon and Nick to see her at the Social Services office at around 7:00 pm that night.

I said "yes" to the appointment. *That was pretty close to bedtime, but it shouldn't take too long should it?*

Jon and Nick and I watched some cartoons after they woke up. I was too riled up on the inside to concentrate on reading even on one of their books. After a time, I turned off the television and asked the boys to pick up the toys while I fixed dinner before heading to Social Services that night.

As I drove to the address I was given, the boys sat in the back seat playing. They seemed calm enough. I guess anywhere we went that wasn't their father's house was okay for them. When we arrived at the building, we were taken to a waiting area before being introduced to a nice lady.

Bernie was of medium height and her soft face was framed by blond-grey curls. Her reading glasses hung from a multi-colored beaded necklace around her neck. She beamed a smile as she introduced herself to Nick and Jon. "Hi Guys! My name is Bernie. Would you like to play in my playroom?"

Her office was set up with a small supervised playroom. A large window looked into the actual office area. The playroom was cozy with lots of toys and of course Lego bricks. A child-sized bookshelf held at least twenty-five or thirty books and was surrounded by miniature bean bag chairs.

After saying hello Bernie pointed to the big window. The boys were quite content to play in the playroom when Bernie and I showed them they could see me at all times. Jon made a beeline to the bookshelf saying "Hey. M…m…Mommy I am big enough to choose my own b…b…book and the chairs are s…s…so cool." Nick toddled off in the other direction.

"Mrs. Phillips," Bernie began.

"Please call me Elizabeth." I interrupted.

"Okay Elizabeth it is," she said with a smile. "Now tell me what's going on that has you concerned?"

I didn't mean to, but I became a machine gun of information.

"The boys don't want to go to their dad's for visitation. Jon started stuttering and said his bottom hurt. Nick still isn't speaking even at almost three years old. Their faces are so sad all the time…" Crying I burbled out. "I haven't hadn't been able to put all the pieces together to protect my sons," I told her. "I truly believe that a relationship with their Dad is extremely important to their development, but I can no longer say with certainty that their father loves them."

Another thought struck me, and I said "You know Greg was not excited about my pregnancy with Jon. And he didn't seem to bond with him though he went through the motions. Greg has always been very self-centered, so I rationalized his lack of enjoyment of his first child to that."

Bernie affirmed me by saying "This is not uncommon, and you can't blame yourself."

Encouraged by her support I shared another experience. "One afternoon I was changing Jon's diaper and talking to him about his new brother or sister that would arrive soon, since I was pregnant with Nick at the time. Greg came in and said the strangest thing.

"'I'm glad Jon's not a girl. I'd be worried about being sexually attracted to her when she got to be a teenager.' At the time I was shocked, but in my confused, abused mind I told myself I should be glad he was sharing his inner feelings and fears with me."

Bernie told me she wanted to interview Jon at that point. She had a feeling that Jon wouldn't be comfortable talking to a 'stranger' by himself so she instructed me before he came in. I was to have him sit on my lap during the interview. I was not to put my arms around him unless absolutely necessary. It was important that I try not to react in any way to things he might say or do. I was to be a *statue* as much as possible.

Waiting in my seat, I watched through the window as Bernie went to get Jon. He looked to me first. I waved and Jon came with her to the office. Nick was engaged and happy. Building something out of Legos with another social worker, he looked up frequently to see me through the window.

Once he was on my lap, Bernie asked, "Jon did you like the playroom?"

Jon said "T...t...there's lots of g...g...great books!"

I smiled but he was in front of me on my lap and didn't see it. I was going to say something about how he was an excellent reader but I remembered I was supposed to be a statue and remained silent.

"Do you know why your mom brought you to see me tonight?"

"She just said we were going to see a nice lady."

"That was very nice. She mentioned that you and your brother don't like to go to your dad's very much."

"I hate D...d...dad," Jon said with vehemence. "He s...s... should go away and never come b...b...back."

With that release of feeling, Jon warmed up to Bernie. He was more open with her that he'd been with me within just a few moments. She had a real gift for working with children in stress, and he began telling her little tidbits about his experience. The more he talked about his Dad and Matt and Sara, the more relaxed his little body became. I wanted to cry feeling his body release the weight of what he'd been holding secret.

He was leaning back against me, when Bernie introduced a therapeutic tool: a male anatomically correct muslin rag doll. It had a simple face and no clothing. There was yarn 'hair' on the head, in the armpits, and the pubic area. When Jon saw it he sat up on my lap no longer relaxed.

Jon became quite animated about this doll, asking why there was no hair on the chest. Bernie asked him about the parts of the doll, starting with the face, arms, and legs. She asked him questions like "Do you suppose he likes ice cream? Do you think he can run fast?"

Eventually and very naturally, she arrived at the genital area. Jon became very aggressive toward the doll, picked it up by the penis and shook it saying, "I told you what would happen if you d-d...didn't do what I told you to!" The longer he held the doll this way the more and more agitated and upset Jon became. He shook the doll so hard; I thought the cloth penis might be ripped off. He put the doll down on the desk and slammed his fist into the belly multiple times, red-faced in anger.

Bernie stopped the interview asking Jon if he would like to play with Nick a little more in the playroom. Jon looked up at me, his face full of sadness mixed with despair and resignation. All he said was "Okay." There was a hopeless aspect to the look on his face and in his eyes. It broke my heart into dozens of jagged shards.

Jon rejoined Nick in the playroom with the other social worker and we waved. As soon as his attention was shifted, Bernie turned away from the window. She looked at me with an intense expression I had not yet seen from her.

"There is some major stuff going on here. I want to go to the police in the city where your ex-husband lives," she said. I was again shocked by the events that now seemed to be hurtling me along out of control.

"Should we make an appointment for tomorrow or something?" I asked.

Bernie's tone was kind, but she was emphatic. "No, we need

to go right now so we have a chance of getting a search warrant for your ex-husband's apartment before he is aware that we know anything has been going on."

Nine o'clock that night we went to the police station near where Greg now lived on the other side of town. It was very quiet in the police station, like an eerie tomb. The heels of my shoes made noise on the polished floor as we were directed down the hall to a conference room.

The ugly metal chairs and utilitarian table in the bare room were well-used and dirty. *I must remember to stop and wash all of our hands before we go home.* The green-grey-brownish metal chairs were freezing so I had one son perched on each knee. *'What is the color on those walls?'* My mind was racing. *Why am I thinking about that now?* I chided myself.

Bernie's basement office must have been furnished with county government-issued furniture but hers was softened and warmed a bit by personal items. In Bernie's office were a silk plant and some photos of family and friends. The room we now occupied at the police station had similar government-issue furniture, but it was as cold as it could be, devoid of all human warmth.

My sons were exhausted. By now it was 10:00pm. Their grand adventure of going to a real police station was wearing thin for them. Bernie and I were quiet, but she smiled encouragement at me from time to time.

Finally, a very young-looking, skinny officer in a navy-blue uniform entered the room.

"Hi, my name is Officer Chris. Can I talk to you guys?"

Nick and Jon looked at him fearfully trying to climb further into my lap. I didn't know at that time that they had been threatened by an imposter in a police-style uniform during the abuse. Fortunately, the officer seemed to be accustomed to talking to children and quickly put them at ease.

Like any child would be, Jon and Nick were very interested in his gun.

Jon asked timidly "C...c...Could we s...s...see your gun?" Nick nodded vigorously to show his interest.

Officer Chris said "You must never play with guns, they're very dangerous. When you are older and grown-up you can take some classes to learn how to properly use and care for a gun." His tone was firm but still kind. "This is a Glock 22," he said holding the gun with great care. I am glad to say I have never had to use it on a person. I have only fired it for practice at the firing range."

I gave the officer all the details I could remember, and Bernie filled in what she had discovered through her interview. Nick and Jon appeared to be ignoring our conversation or maybe they were exhausted or shut down emotionally. My tired overwrought mind was wandering again. *How did we end up in this frigid room with its cold, dirty furniture talking to a police officer in the middle of the night?* I wanted to cry, to scream, to run away from the new reality that my sons had been living in for quite some time. I could do none of those things at that moment though. I didn't want to frighten Jon and Nick. Their tenuous security lay in my ability to remain strong and calm. I felt chilled to the bone even with my jacket on. We should all have been in our warm safe beds by then.

After Bernie, Officer Chris. and I talked, we let the boys tell of the things they experienced including the amazing toy room at Miss Bernie's office. The officer was kind and efficient. Though it felt like hours, we were only there for about ninety minutes.

Suddenly we were done. Bernie hoped the court would execute a search warrant early the next day. She had scheduled an emergency hearing for the following morning. The hope was to set legal proceedings in motion so Jon and Nick wouldn't have to go for their upcoming weekend visit.

"The initial, temporary, seven-day restraining order should keep them safe for the next week," she explained. Much later we found out that it had, in fact, saved their lives.

Bernie told me to go home and she would call me tomorrow.

Go home? It didn't seem safe to go home or anywhere else for that matter.

In my most frightened imaginings I had not anticipated the depth of the abuse my sons had endured. Though I didn't know it at the time, my horrendous new understanding from Bernie's appointment and the Police visit was just the tip of the iceberg. I felt like my heart had been ripped from my chest and stuck back in with careless, hasty, cold hands.

I was frightened because Nick and Jon were scheduled to visit their Dad for the weekend in just three days. *What if the court refused to issue the restraining order? What if they thought all this was my fault?* I had planned Jon's birthday party for Friday evening, and they were supposed to go home with their Dad for the weekend after the party. *'What am I going to do?'* I thought. *Where can we hide?* I felt like I was coming apart at the seams.

I reminded myself I didn't want to frighten my two brave sons, so I put on as normal a face as I could manage. We stopped at the bathroom on the way out and washed our hands. Then we left the police station. The parking lot was deserted but I looked all around ready to run back into the station if I saw anything.

We made it to the car and the boys were asleep almost as soon as I strapped them into their car seats. As I drove home thoughts raged through my mind. *How did this happen? Why didn't I know sooner? With all the pornography, strip clubs, sexual and emotional abuse I had endured, I still couldn't believe he had done harm to our sons.* I had feared something was wrong with Greg's relationship with the boys, but I had no idea.

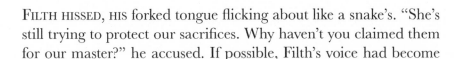

FILTH HISSED, HIS forked tongue flicking about like a snake's. "She's still trying to protect our sacrifices. Why haven't you claimed them for our master?" he accused. If possible, Filth's voice had become even more sinister. For half a second, he wondered if this was how Mire felt.

Stench left the cavern room to search for and attempt to claim the two boys yet again. He had no idea where to look first.

WHAT AM I supposed to do now? What about work? I fretted. I didn't want to let Nick and Jon out of my sight for a moment. Though the apartment was securely locked when we arrived I checked each room of the small apartment before letting go of the boys' hands. They went right back to sleep after being put in their cribs.

I lay in bed staring at the ceiling trying to wrap my mind around what I had learned this night. It was impossible to comprehend. The first of many *why* prayers made its way to God's throne. Finally, I was mentally emotionally and physically wrung out. Sleep claimed what parts of my brain it could. I rested in fits and starts, plagued by weird dreams.

CHAPTER 5

DID LAST NIGHT *really happen? What day is this? Wednesday, yeah, Wednesday.*
Slivers of pre-dawn light came through the mini blinds of my bedroom window as I got up. It was freezing in my room. Another February day. I jumped back into bed and snuggled deep into my down comforter. Exhausted from a fitful night's sleep, I thought, *there is no way I wanted to let the boys out of my sight, much less go to work.*

This time when I got up, I put on my fluffy, pink robe and warm, winter slippers. I crossed the hall, quiet, as I peeped into their bedroom. They were sprawled in their cribs, sound asleep, covers askew because their blanket sleepers were evidently warm enough. I even heard Nick's little snore. It sounded like a tiny choo-choo train and made me feel an extra pang of love for him. His snoring certainly wasn't annoying like an adult's. Jon was wearing his favorite Tigger blanket sleeper. They were so small. My heart broke to know they had been abused.

Later that morning, Jon and Nick sat at the coffee table, working on their coloring books with great industry. The sun coming in the front windows was warm and felt good. I was looking at a magazine, half-thinking about the boy's lunch when the ringing of the phone startled me.

"Mrs. Phillips?"

"Yes, this is she," I responded. I was hesitant to give too much information because I didn't recognize the voice.

"This is Bernie, your Social Worker, remember? I promised you a call today."

"Of course," I said, recalling the previous night. "Thank you for calling, Bernie. Please call me Elizabeth."

"We are scheduled for an emergency hearing tomorrow afternoon at one pm. Do you know where the courthouse is for Slate county?"

"Yes, I believe so, but I'll check my map. Do the boys have to be there?"

"Absolutely not," she said with a stern tone. "Please, don't bring them. I'm not sure if the search warrant was executed this morning or not. I hope they did, so any evidence can be collected before your ex-husband knows we are onto him." Her matter-of-fact tone of voice saddened me as I realized she had to deal with this often enough that it didn't faze her anymore. *How can she do this work, day in and day out with one family after another?*

"I doubt he is," I said to her. "I'm sure Greg would have called me raging about the search warrant if the police had gone to his door."

After lunch, I was as quiet as I could be when I closed the door to the boys' bedroom. When I knew they were both sound asleep for their afternoon nap, I went to the kitchen to use the phone. With a heart that felt like lead, I dialed my parents' phone number. *How could I break this horrible news to them?* The phone rang several times before I heard my mom's voice.

"Hello?"

"Hi Mom," was all I could get out before I dissolved in tears.

"Honey, what's wrong?" she said, starting to panic with me. "Are you all right? Are Jon and Nick okay?"

Trying hard to stop crying, I said, "Is Daddy home? Can you

both get on the phone?" I didn't want to repeat this. Going through it once was horrible enough.

"Elizabeth, what's wrong?" Daddy said, getting on the upstairs phone in their home.

"Greg has been," I forced it out, "abusing the boys."

My mother was the first to speak after a long moment of shock. "Seriously? Are you sure?" She, like I, was in absolute horror.

Standing in the kitchen shaking, I reached for a tissue. I sat on the floor as much as the phone cord allowed. "Don't you remember how weird they looked at Christmas. When we took them to lunch? It broke my heart to take them back to Greg's apartment. I felt like I was abandoning them. My voice, along with the rest of my body, was shaking as I talked.

"That was the only thing you could do," Daddy said.

Remember when Jon started stuttering and complained about his bottom hurting? Why didn't I figure this out sooner? We went to Social Services last night and a very nice social worker, named Bernie interviewed the boys. She took us directly to the police station in the area where Greg lives. The police did an interview with me, the boys, and Bernie. Then they sent us home." I suddenly felt more tired than I could ever remember being. *It actually feels good to share this burden with people who love Jon and Nick. But now it was theirs too, and that made me sad.*

"What did the boys say?" Mom asked.

"They talked about bad things happening at their dad's apartment and someplace else. Some of the 'bad things' constitute sexual abuse. They are so scared they will have to go back there. We have an emergency hearing set for tomorrow to hopefully make sure they don't have to go on this coming weekend's visit."

My dad was never as quiet as when he was angry. He was exceptionally quiet right now. We waited for him to speak, keeping our conversation to a minimum while he formed his thoughts. "We will fly down," he said suddenly. "But I don't think we can get there before the hearing."

"I would love to see you so much, but I may need you more, later on. From what Bernie says, this hearing is a slam dunk. I'm still a little worried, but I am not going to let Greg hurt them any more! I'll do whatever it takes. I'm sure they will stop this weekend's visit. Greg will be so embarrassed; he will stay away forever. Jim and Brenda are bringing the girls and coming down. Jim will go with me to court and Brenda will watch the kids. I'll call to keep you informed when the boys are sleeping. I love you both very much!"

"We love you, Honey!"

"I hear Jon talking to himself, so he is awake, and Nick will be shortly. I'll talk to you soon. Bye-bye." I hung up the phone, heading toward the boys' room as I dried the remnants of my tears. I had little hope in the face of such evil days.

Thursday dawn came after a night of little sleep. *Today is the hearing. What will happen, I wonder?* Even though it was still early, I got up to start the day. No use trying to relax. Best get a move on. *I don't want this morning to be any more hectic than necessary.*

"But, Mommy, why can't we go with you?" Jon said. Nick was starting to cry. They were somewhat mollified when I told them that Uncle Jim was going with me to court. "Besides, Aunt Brenda will take care of you and your cousins here at our house. You always have fun playing with your cousins."

I was nauseous, frightened, and so fatigued that I wasn't sure I could put one foot in front of the other. *I can't imagine having to go through this by myself.* I looked out the window, thinking about all the people supporting me; Social Services, the police, my parents praying for us. They were right there, standing, waiting with me. I was so grateful. *I don't want to face Greg, but at least Bernie will be there with Jim and me.*

It was quiet on the drive to the county courthouse. Jim's car was comfortable and warm, but my heart was cold with fear. Neither one of us had any idea what to expect. *Who, in a million years, ever expects to have to go court for something like this?*

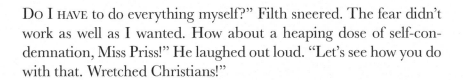

Do I HAVE to do everything myself?" Filth sneered. The fear didn't work as well as I wanted. How about a heaping dose of self-condemnation, Miss Priss!" He laughed out loud. "Let's see how you do with that. Wretched Christians!"

JIM WAS FURIOUS with Greg. He was practically shaking with it as we drove toward the courthouse. He whispered something under his breath and hit the steering wheel. I couldn't understand it all, but it sounded like he was considering serious bodily harm to Greg.

"No!" I replied. "He's not worth your future."

"He's not worth the air he's breathing," Jim said, his voice a snarl.

I told Jim God would handle Greg, and he seemed to put his rage on the back burner to some extent. *As always, I was praying that Jon and Nick would be kept safe.* A seed of condemnation was just starting to develop in me. I felt my neck tense up and my hands felt cold inside my gloves. Like a tsunami, the doubts assailed me. *How could I have let this happen? Why didn't I do something sooner? Why hadn't God answered a multitude of requests to keep Jon and Nick safe while they were with their dad? Why didn't I figure it out sooner? Why was I still so afraid of Greg?* Nausea was coming up again.

To stop the flood of questions in my mind, I focused my gaze out the car window. *Some snow would really improve this landscape*, I thought. *Lonely grey skies and brown fields as far as the eye can see; suits my mood.* It was freezing out with few cars on the road. *Would this be easier if it was sunny and the fields were green with crops? I don't think so.*

"Thanks again, Jim, for picking me up and taking me to this hearing. It really helps to have you here," I said, hoping his mood had changed.

"No problem," Jim replied with a short tone. He was still angry, but much calmer.

Please bless him, Lord, I prayed silently. This took a massive chunk out of his day. He drove from his home past the turnoff to the courthouse to drop Brenda and the girls at my place, then back to the courthouse. And after court, he would reverse the process. He will have driven over one-hundred-fifty miles by the time he and Brenda and the kids get home. I knew he'd go back to his office and work until his day's work is finished. *I wish there was something I could do to make it up to them.*

I felt my stomach clench when we rounded the corner and the courthouse came into view. *Uh-oh!* My nausea became worse, filling my chest and throat. I almost asked Jim to pull over.

"I'm so glad the boys don't have to be here for this," I said as we pulled into the parking lot. I was surprised and relieved the words came out. *Those doors make this ugly granite building look like a cave,* I thought. *It's a little scary, even for me.* We crunched across the bitter cold parking lot towards the dark entrance. Once inside, we checked through security and the metal detector, I felt frozen. Even my eyes were watering from the cold—or was it tears? Bernie told me to appear as composed as I could manage.

Jim and I sat in the hall of the courthouse on a freezing, stone bench. No one else we knew had arrived yet. People moved around in the hallway, courtroom doors opened and closed, a couple of attorneys stood down the hall in deep discussion. Lots of activity on this day in the courthouse. Bernie and one of her colleagues came in shortly after that and I was relieved to see her. But I felt so dazed and sick to my stomach it seemed like I wasn't really a part of what was transpiring. Bernie didn't seem worried as she sat, chatting with her colleague. I felt as though I was moving through the scene in slow motion while everyone and everything else moved at full speed around me.

Greg had not appeared yet, although Bernie told me she had spoken with him early in the morning to tell him about the hearing this afternoon. *I am so glad I didn't have to see or confront him, but I am surprised that he didn't show up for something this important.*

Bernie's colleague stayed with Jim and me while Bernie went into the courtroom to speak with the judge. She came back out and said, "Elizabeth, you can come in now."

"May I have my brother come in as well?"

She held the door open, shaking my brother's hand as we entered. "You must be Jim," she said with a smile.

The judge was very solemn as he told us that he had issued an emergency protective order for seven days. Their father was not to come anywhere near them during that time. I felt like I had been holding my breath, and now I could relax a little.

As we walked the hall, Bernie said, "I will call to inform Greg of the order this afternoon. After my conversation with him this morning, I'm not looking forward to it." She smiled. "But it's part of the job." I looked at her, feeling a new sense of worry. *What if this whole situation was putting her in danger? I'd never forgive myself.*

She seemed to see my concern and patted me on the shoulder. "Don't worry," she said, trying to reassure me. My face must have been scared. "I'll be very sure he understands completely. The court will mail a copy of the order to his home, but it will be several days before he receives it."

When we left the courthouse, I finally felt sure I wasn't going to throw up and I could breathe freely again. It seemed even the atmosphere in the hallway was lighter as we exited. I was so relieved; I felt the weight of a mountain had been removed from my shoulders.

Jim and I drove back to my home in much better spirits. *Seven days isn't very long,* I thought, *but it will keep them safe this weekend.* It also included the party I had planned for Jon's fourth birthday the next night. *What a relief!*

I was so anxious to see and hug them, the drive home seemed like it took forever.

CHAPTER 6

IWANTED JON AND Nick within arm's reach at all times if possible. *What was going on?* I had no idea where the unnamed fear was coming from. It caused me to wake up several times a night to check on my boys like that nightmare was real. *What is wrong with me?* I kept thinking throughout the day. *I am so glad I purchased gifts and party supplies last week. I don't want to go anywhere today.*

BRRING! BRRING! The phone jumped from the wall into my eardrum. Wow, that startled me. I hoped it didn't wake the boys from their naps.

"Hello?" I answered.

"Elizabeth this is Bonnie," the voice replied. My mother-in-law! *What does she want?* I wondered if Greg told her about the hearing yesterday.

"Hi Bonnie, what's up?" I tried to keep my voice light and civil.

"You aren't still going to have the birthday party tonight, are you?" I'd better be careful what I said to her but I was getting annoyed.

"Why do you think I would cancel Jon's party? He's been looking forward to it for weeks."

"I think," she started with a superior tone "since his dad can't be there because of the court stuff it wouldn't be good for you to have it." *What did Greg tell her?* I wondered.

55

"I won't disappoint Jon. Greg cannot attend that is true. But you are still invited."

"Well I guess I'll see you tonight." She rushed off the phone.

I had to wonder what she knew. She sounded so clueless. And she was thinking more about her adult son's feelings than the feelings of her almost-four-year-old grandson. My hands shook with anger as I put down the phone. *Is it possible that Greg was abused and she is in complete denial?* I considered. *Another mystery...*

I enjoyed baking and decorating Jon's birthday cake while the boys were napping. Later that day we had a great time at his party. Greg's mom did show up, as did Greg's dad with his third wife in tow. My friends from Bible study came with their kids. My fellow moms from the Christian mother's co-op came with their spouses and kids. Jim and Brenda drove down with my nieces. Looking around I was happy to see such a great turnout. *This is quite a houseful, but I think everybody is having a good time. Jon is livelier than I have seen him in a while.*

Brenda whispered in my ear "You're giving an Academy Award-winning performance, especially with Jon and Nick's grandparents here. I don't know how you do it." She gave me a hug.

"Thanks, I just wanted it to be fun, especially for Jon."

As my good friend Susan left, she put some dollar bills in my pocket. She had been praying for us since I told her of my concerns several weeks ago.

All the guests left, and Jim and Brenda took Jon and Nick home with them to stay for the weekend as I was scheduled to work. This was God's provision for the boys' care since I had to work Saturday and Sunday. I normally only worked the weekends that the boys went to their dad's house.

As I wandered aimlessly around our small apartment my mind whirled as I got ready for bed. I felt exhausted and alone. I started to cry as I took down my hair. I kept asking God "Why did this happen? What am I going to do?"

Working part-time I was just barely making it financially. Did I need a lawyer? How would I pay for one? What about the counseling I knew would be necessary? How in the world would I pay for that?"

As I slipped off my jeans the bills Susan slipped into my pocket tumbled onto the floor. At the time I thought she had given me twenty or twenty-five much appreciated dollars. When I picked it up I started counting. It was $500! Susan and her husband had young children and she was staying home with them. How in the world could she possibly afford to just give this to me? She already told me she didn't expect to be repaid. She was adamant it was a gift.

I heard God's still small gentle whisper in my mind "You and the boys will be cared for."

The 35-mile commute to work the next day was nerve-wracking. I was frightened to death. Somehow, I was convinced that all the drivers around me knew that I had $500 in my purse. I was driving in the dark on an early Saturday morning in the seamier part of downtown to get to work. I deposited the cash later in the day at the Credit Union without incident, but I was a nervous wreck until I did. Fortunately, work was slow, as I was having a very hard time concentrating.

I breathed a sigh of relief as I finished my shift on Sunday. It felt wonderful to be able to drive to Jim and Brenda's and pick up my sons. I was so happy to see Nick and Jon. And they had a good time over the weekend with their aunt, uncle, and cousins. That, too, blessed me.

Thus began the rhythm of our lives post revelation.

CHAPTER 7

W ITH TREPIDATION AND a shaking right hand I opened the
door on the small house at the address I had been given.
It appeared to be a residence that had been converted
into a psychologist's office. It still shocked me to know this was all
really happening.

The office is quite cozy and warm I thought as we entered. I
overheard the woman at the front speaking with another patient
bolstering my peace. *The receptionist seems very kind. That's a good sign*
I thought my fears slightly abated.

As she finished with the patient ahead of us, she looked at me.
"I'm Wendy, Dr. Perez's receptionist," she said. Speaking directly to
the boys she said "Hi Guys! Would you like to play with some of the
toys over here?" She was cheerful as she indicated a corner of the
waiting room.

Jon said "I...Is it OK M...m...Mommy?" Nick as usual stood
behind him looking on and nodding.

"Sure," I said, "I'll be right here filling out paperwork."
Impressed that she addressed Jon and Nick directly. *I have a good
feeling about this place.*

The door to the inner office opened and a middle-aged man
strode through the doorway with joyful energy. He was slightly
taller than average with thick dark hair and coffee-colored eyes. His
polo-type shirt and chino slacks exuded a relaxed but professional

air. As he walked into the waiting room, he extended his hand to me. "I'm Dr. Perez," he said with a smile.

"Hello I'm Elizabeth. And this is Jon, and this is Nick," I said noting how they had looked up with apprehension from their play. They were startled to hear the unfamiliar male voice. They looked at Dr. Perez with frank suspicion in their eyes. "Guys this is Dr. Perez can you shake his hand please?" I said smiling to encourage them. "That's the way," I said as they reluctantly complied.

"I have more toys in here," Dr. Perez stated indicating his office. "Mom can wait for you out here," he said firmly.

What? Wait...this doesn't feel right I thought all the while smiling at them to encourage them to go ahead. *I'm glad the recommendation for Dr. Perez came from Bernie* I thought, feeling troubled. *I just sent them into a closed room with a man I just met.* Then I realized my anxiety had to do with being out of visual contact with them for the first time since the hearing.

I heard Wendy say something to me. "Would you like a cup of water?"

"Ye...yes please," I stammered, still staring at the now-closed inner office door. I went back to the paperwork with difficulty. *I still don't know how I'm going to pay for this* I thought.

"Here you go," Wendy said as she gave me the water and an encouraging smile.

"Thank you," I replied looking up from the paperwork. She was caring for me while the boys were with the doctor. I really appreciated her efforts to distract me from my worries, though they weren't working very well.

I finished the paperwork and returned the clipboard to Wendy. *If we come back here regularly, I'll have to bring a project to work on while I'm waiting. I'm too distracted to read.* I mused. "Maybe a needle-point..." I started to say to myself.

Suddenly the inner office door opened. *Finally,* I thought. My relief felt like a cool breeze on a warm day, almost palpable.

The boys came out and Jon said "T...t...That was fun M...m... Mommy." Nick nodded his agreement vigorously.

Mr. Perez smiled and said, "Yeah come on in Mom and see what we've been doing." Nick grabbed my hand and pulled me toward the office.

"Wow, what a great ranch!" I said examining the meticulously set up horses, cows, cowboys, wagon, and stagecoach with its own horses. *Jon seems a little subdued. I wonder why?* I watched him with some concern.

"How are you doing Jon?" I asked him.

"Okay. D...D...Dr. Perez told us we could t...t...tell him anything," Jon said, his expression guarded. "Jon and Nick why don't you play in here a little longer while I talk to your Mom," Dr. Perez stated matter-of-factly. Standing in the hall Dr. Perez closed, but did not latch the inner office door, and said in a low voice "Your sons are terrified of something or someone."

Elizabeth Anne, don't you dare cry I told myself.

"Yes, I know," I answered, tears threatening. "But I'm not sure who or what happened to them while they were with their father."

Dr. Perez nodding said "I'd like to see them on a weekly basis. Will that be possible?"

"Yes absolutely," I responded. *Not sure how I'm going to pay for it though.*

"Great, have Wendy make an appointment for next week," he said.

"Okay ah... do you have any questions for me?" I asked, wondering why I wasn't being consulted here. Social Services and the police were very interested in what I had to tell them.

Dr. Perez smiling sympathetically said "No, not today but I will let you know."

"All right," I said. *Nice place,* I thought to myself as I helped the boys put on their jackets.

"Jon interrupted my thoughts by asking "M…m…Mommy are we going to M…M… McDonald's?"

I remembered to respond with enthusiasm. I told them we might go thinking that it would make the weekly counseling appointments something to which they would look forward.

"Yes, we are!"

AROUND THE SMALL, dingy, darkened room there was sinister murmuring. Occasionally a demonic cackle rang out, often followed by the thud of a body landing heavily on the floor. Soot was everywhere.

The room became silent as a large, black, forbidding form entered the room. Terror dripped from the walls falling on everyone present. The recently entered demon, Filth swung his horrible huge head around to ascertain that everyone in the room had bowed in obeisance.

"As you are all well aware our master seeks two little blond boys for his pleasure. Not just any two boys but particular innocents. The more times you have tried and failed to obtain them the more he wants these two. Their meddling mother and her church people have caused one failure after another. We have been rebuffed time after time in our efforts," he spat contemptuously and continued "We now have another problem. The mother is seeing a Christian counselor who is powerful in discernment and difficult to trick. She is teaching this pathetic weakling of a mother how to do spiritual battle effectively. An even bigger problem is the boys are now seeing a very skilled therapist. They may well start talking. The dad and his local group of idiots abused them physically and sexually. Our master did not command this. He would have been better served by keeping their innocence intact.

"Since the adults in this group of slime bags couldn't control themselves the mother and her people will have a viable case to influence the court. The court has always been an area of strength for us but the information those brats are telling will be hard for our people to deflect. If the court denies unsupervised visitation with their father that will put these two hated preys temporarily out of reach, and you will continue to suffer the master's wrath!" Filth's voice was fueled with anger and disgust. "Since the idiotic father and his inept group have been totally ineffectual, we are going to have to take a more active role than we have up until now. We need to get rid of the therapist seeing the boys before anyone protecting the mom and her children can extend any more protection around him! Do you fools not understand this!?"

One of the underlings spoke up. "Perhaps," he said with a timid voice "the replacements would still suit the master."

The giant demon's eyes flashed red hot in anger. "You weren't paying attention!" Filth roared. "I just told you that the master wants *these* boys more than ever because of all the failures to obtain them. You fool! You are not fit even to move the dung heaps. BE GONE!"

A small clink sounded as the underling disappeared and the crystal dangling from its neck fell to the floor. In an instant the cannibalistic group began fighting, biting screaming and scrambling to grab the stone.

Stumpy sooty wings and bodies spread even more black debris around the cave. One of the demons came up chortling the hard-earned prize held by the chain in a misshapen clawed hand.

Filth backhanded him across the room.

"ENOUGH!" he roared.

CHAPTER 8

"**I** CAN HARDLY BELIEVE it Elizabeth. I am so sorry," my long-time friend said over the phone.

"I know Barb. It's so awful," I said.

"Are you all safe?" Barb inquired with anxiety in her voice.

"I think so, but the police have said unofficially that I should make myself and the boys scarce."

"Well, come down here for a night or two. Your ex-husband doesn't know me or where I live. My kids would love it. We can have a slumber party," she said, her tone turning bright.

"I can't even tell you how good that sounds. I especially appreciate your willingness to have us visit," I said, feeling a little tearful.

"Of course, come on over," she said warmly. "Here are the directions to my new place." *She was recently divorced,* and I got excited as I hung up the phone and went into the boys' bedroom.

"Hey Guys! We're going to a friend of Mommy's to spend the night. She has kids about your ages, and it'll be fun!"

Despite my cheerful tone Jon and Nick looked at each other then at me. They did not seem pleased or excited. They looked worried. Suddenly I realized why.

"Okay, come here please," I requested as I sat down in the rocking chair. They complied but very slowly. I set one son on each knee and asked, "What's wrong?"

Jon and Nick looked at each other and then Jon said slowly

"T...t...That's what D...d...Dad used to say and we *had* to go. That's w-w-when the bad s-s-stuff happened."

Internally horrified, I did my best to keep the emotions from my face and said, "Oh guys, I am so sorry," I said feeling disgust and rage flare up. I pushed it down and said, "Here's what we can do; we'll go, then you can meet her and her kids. And if you feel the least bit scared or uncomfortable you just whisper in my ear and we'll leave immediately. I promise."

Still unsure, and struggling to overcome their fear, Nick and Jon nodded their assent. *We need to have a good time* I thought *to start replacing some of the bad memories.* It took us a few moments to get ready and in the car. But soon enough we were on our way. Both boys were silent on the ride across town to Barb's home. I had no way to warn Barb about the possibility that their behavior might not be what she expected.

Oh well I thought. *She's a great friend. I've known her since junior high and I know it will be fine.* I turned my thoughts to God in a hasty prayer. *Please help us have a good time Lord.*

We arrived at her townhouse to see her two kids looking out the front window waiting for us. *A good start* I thought.

Barb came to the door with an armful of toys. "Hi Jon! Hi Nick!" When she saw their faces, she toned down her excitement. "These are for you," she said with a gentler tone. Somehow, she had managed to get new stuffed animals and some toy cars for my sons in a really short period of time.

Her kids were very excited and said, "C'mon, come see our playhouse." Nick and Jon looked at me for permission. I said "Sure. Have fun," and off they went down the hall, happily chatting.

I looked at Barb and almost cried. "Thank you so much. I haven't been able to relax in weeks."

"Let's get something to drink. Do you still like diet pop?"

"That would be great."

We went into the kitchen and sat down. As I listened out for the boys' voices, I filled her in on recent events in my life. I told her about the visit to Social Services, the police station, and the first hearing at court. She was stunned. Her blue eyes were full of tears almost as soon as I started talking.

After a half-hour or so she said "Let me check on the kids. You sit here and relax a minute." She went down the hall and I heard some laughter. She returned and said "They are having a terrific time. Should we get pizza for dinner?"

"That sounds wonderful."

I was actually feeling a little sleepy sitting with Barb. It had been so long since I'd been able to relax my vigilance about everything that I was physically fatigued. Once I relaxed that tiny bit I fell into a sound sleep sitting straight up in her kitchen chair.

I was awakened with a start by the doorbell. I heard Barb say "Thank you," and close the door.

"Pizza's here!" she called from the door.

All four kids came running down the hall sliding in their stockinged feet on the hardwood floor. I laughed out loud. "Great game," I said to no one in particular. We sat at the table as Barb served slices of pizza on colorful plates from her pantry. The pizza was delicious—piping hot with lots of cheese and pepperoni. Or maybe it was my relaxed state that helped me actually taste what I ate.

"Barb this pizza is the best I've ever had."

"Good friends and good food," she said. "And I have ice cream for dessert."

The children were ecstatic and dove into their bowls with delight. The ice cream was Nick's favorite flavor, chocolate chip. Jon enjoyed it too. We picked up our dishes and took them to the kitchen.

"Don't worry about those, we'll take care of them later," Barb said. "Now let's get pajamas on and brush teeth. Then we can watch a movie. I rented *Dumbo*.

Barb is amazing I thought. *When did she have time to buy toys, get ice cream, and rent a movie?* I took the boys in the bathroom to change and brush their teeth. While there I whispered "Is everything okay? Do you want to leave?" Jon and Nick looked at me a little surprised. Then Jon said, "No, we're having fun," and Nick nodded.

"All right as long as you two are doing alright," I said. They both smiled at me. I had not seen them this relaxed in a long time.

We all snuggled up on sleeping bags and comforters on the floor to watch *Dumbo*. I struggled but failed to keep my eyes open. I vaguely heard the sound of trumpets in the movie. Dumbo was on a high tower supposed to dive into a small tub of water and the ringmaster said "And now the climax of our show..."

Suddenly Jon was in my lap trying to bury his head under my arm. "Jon what's wrong?" I asked confused and disturbed by his reaction.

"M...m...Mommy he said 'c...c...climax' in the movie. Why is that in a cartoon?" Jon asked in tears.

I was befuddled and wasn't sure how to answer. "Have you heard that word before?" I asked then chided myself.

Stupid question.

Jon looked upset and slightly scared. "Yeah, we...we...we aren't s -s-supposed to s -s- say t-t-th-th-hat," he said, his stuttering suddenly worse. In a flash I figured it out.

"Jon, Nick, let me explain..." I started to say. Nick covered his ears with his hands. I gently pulled them away from his ears a little bit and said "Sometimes a word can have more than one meaning. In the cartoon the climax of the show means the best, most exciting part of the show. Did you see Dumbo fly with his big silly ears?" I said. They looked at the TV and then at me. I encouraged them with my smile and relaxed tone. It took a minute but both boys calmed down.

Once again, I was furious inside and all relaxation was gone from my body.

Barb returned from putting her kids to bed. Jon and Nick curled themselves up in their sleeping bags on either side of me sound asleep. Barb looked at me quizzically.

"This is my life these days," my tone flat.

Barb asked in a soft voice "What was that all about?"

"Let's talk in the kitchen," I said, extricating myself so I could stand up and stretch. The boys slept on as we left the room.

"I don't really know what is going on. I can only surmise that my sons are somehow familiar with the sexual connotation of the word 'climax.' Jon and Nick must have been warned not to say the word or anything about it." My stomach started turning flips. "Their innocence and childhood have been stolen from them physically and emotionally," I said, enraged yet sad. "My ex-husband used to look at pornography all the time so maybe that's where they were exposed to it," I thought aloud.

Barb looked ready to cry. "Oh Elizabeth," she said "I am so very sorry. Whatever I can do please let me know."

"I will. I promise. Tonight has been a huge help. You have no idea how much. Thank you."

I slept better that night than I had since this living nightmare started. Barb was up when Jon's and Nick's voices woke me—they were having fun and laughing!

Barb fixed an excellent breakfast for us. After that we reluctantly headed home.

I was now convinced we needed to move to hide from Greg. *But where? And how?* I felt sure no matter where we went Greg would find us.

God help us.

CHAPTER 9

"**H**EY GUYS, WAIT for me," I said as I struggled with the finicky apartment door lock. I was frazzled this Sunday morning.

As usual I thought.

I had heard the enemy was always very busy on Sunday mornings, as families got ready to go to church. I could really believe it, especially today. I wanted to set a good example for my sons by being peaceful and calm as we set out for church. I wanted to praise God and sing worship songs we knew with the radio, giving Satan no room to mess with us. But today I wasn't loving or worshipful.

Instead I was running late, angry about a small lost shoe. We eventually found it, but then there was a spilled bowl of cereal and milk and a complete change of clothing for Nick. I let the spilled milk stay on the table, rushing to get out the door.

Feeling nauseous and guilty with myself for once again yelling at my two young sons I apologized to them. And all this turmoil for what; just so we can get to church to make a joyful noise unto the Lord?

Really nice Elizabeth!

As I strapped Jon and Nick into their car seats I apologized again. We started off and I turned on our favorite radio station. While we rode along, we sang worship songs along with the radio. The day started to look better. The sky was a blue so intense it was almost tinged with violet. What a gorgeous autumn Sunday. The leaves danced in their colorful wardrobe tickled by a soft breeze. And the breeze kept the brilliant sunshine from being too hot. Still the day was warm enough to confirm winter wasn't even a thought yet.

I gave a little sigh of contentment until I glanced down at the dashboard. The gas gauge showed we were running on fumes.

Oh no I thought. *Our church is still 35 minutes away. I don't have time to stop and get gas now.* My sigh of contentment turned into a slight gasp of frustration. *Oh, why did I decide to go to a church so far away anyway?*

Because I asked you to, the still small voice spoke in my brain.

What if I run out of gas on the freeway? I thought, starting to feel panic rise as tension in my shoulders.

The soft voice said *Trust Me. Don't be afraid.*

I brushed that thought away and continued in panic mode.

And yet we made it. All the way on fumes.

Whew, that was close, I thought as I made it to the parking lot. I had been so tense, I felt physically worn down. It was almost as if I'd pushed the car there with my frail, pale arms. But my sons dozed peacefully in the backseat. They seemed to have the *trust thing* all figured out.

They were such a blessing!

"Thanks for getting us here safely Lord," I breathed.

They woke up as I unbuckled them happy with both the brief nap and our destination. "I'm excited about S...s...Sunday S...s... school today M...m...Mommy!" Jon exclaimed.

"That's great honey. What are you looking forward to?"

"We're going to have a puppet s...s...show. And play with clay!!"

"Wow sounds like fun!"

"How about you Nick?"

Nick murmured something to Jon who promptly announced, "They have an awesome train set in his class,"

"Cool!" I replied.

The building for Sunday School (pre-school to sixth grade) was across the street from the sanctuary and nursery. We dropped Jon off at his classroom with a spring in our step.

"Bye Jon, have fun, see you after church," I said. Nick waved.

We turned and walked away preparing to cross the busy street to the other part of the church. This morning I insisted that we hold hands to cross at the traffic light. He did not always want to hold my hand and when he didn't, we compromised on his holding onto the shoulder strap on my purse except when crossing streets.

Nick was strong-willed even as a baby. I firmly believed that the Lord and I could channel that trait into tenacity as he grew. In the meantime, we had some interesting conversations..

I continued to fuss and fume in my brain still feeling guilty about the rough start to our morning. The still small voice spoke in my mind again and said *I love you.*

Seriously that can't be possible after my behavior this morning I thought. I dismissed that love as impossible and stewed in my guilt.

Nick and I arrived at the curb to wait for the traffic light. I looked down and to my left where my son was standing. Nick wasn't paying any attention to me but had still stuck his hand up absolutely confident I would be there. He knew I would guide him safely across the street.

As I gazed at that little arm in the air clad in his favorite red blazer, I realized something. That small gesture from my young child showed me in a short moment everything God had been trying to show me all morning.

I am here. Trust Me. I love you. I'll be with you and keep you safe.

I almost started to cry. I had a lot to think about during and after church.

After the service we got gas for the car and a bottle of pop for each of us for the trip home. Later that afternoon the phone rang while Nick and Jon were napping. As usual I stiffened with alarm as

I went to answer it. Phone calls were often bad news except at the times my parents called.

To my relief it was my friend Susan. It was good to talk to her and it was nice to hear her care and concern as she asked after us.

"Oh we're fine. I'm sorry you were worried. We went to see a friend and stayed the other night," I told her.

"I got concerned when I couldn't reach you on the phone. Are you sure it is safe at your friend's place?" Susan asked.

"I think so," I said thinking about the night at Barb's. But I'm beginning to look into women's shelters or someplace similar for us to hide out."

"Well I don't know how you feel about this, but Chuck and I discussed it, and you guys are welcome to come to stay in our basement," she said with a question in her voice.

"Oh my gosh, are you sure?" I asked knowing she had struggled with almost debilitating anxiety and fear for some time.

"Yes," she said firmly. "It's just a basement, but I think you would be safe here. The boys' father doesn't know us and you wouldn't have utility bills he could track."

"That's true," I said, the realization and joy rising in my throat. "God bless you!" I said feeling hopeful for the first time in a long time. I thanked God for his provision and then started considering details. *How will I get my mail without filing a change of address to Chuck and Susan's? That would defeat the purpose of the move. I can get a post office box near work.* I needed to continue working, especially with the counseling expenses coming up. I could have Maria, my babysitter come to Susan's and Chuck's house, instead of the apartment and hoped being in hiding would alleviate her fears a bit.

The following Saturday, Jim, Brenda, and my friends from Bible study loaded a truck with our belongings and furniture.

We left behind my answering machine with an active apartment phone line. They would remain there for the last six weeks of my lease. I'm not sure I would have thought of leaving the phone there, so it must have been Holy Spirit giving me direction.

We drove in a caravan over to Susan and Chuck's house. I drove with one eye on the rear-view mirror to be sure I wasn't followed. I didn't want Greg to show up and know what was going on.

Chuck met us in the driveway and handed me a remote garage door opener. I was so blessed by this, especially when I discovered that he had installed it just for my family. Having that remote made it possible to duck into the garage when we arrived home, quickly and safely, successful in hiding my car from view.

I was expecting a damp, concrete basement with exposed pipes, but what I found was God's overabundant provision. Two bedrooms, a bathroom, and a living room—all furnished, warm and cozy.

CHAPTER 10

"WELL OF COURSE I understand, but I am sad," I told Maria. "I asked you for a six-month commitment and you have fulfilled that very well. I hate to lose you! You do a terrific job and the boys are crazy about you. We will all miss you. I understand your fear, though. Besides college is important and you need to have some time for fun, as well as study," I told her with a wink.

After she walked out the door I thought, *now what will I do?* Having Maria care for the boys in our own place had been so wonderful. I mused with a twinge of panic. *Who can I trust to care for the boys while I work?*

"Help me Lord! Please help! I am desperate here Lord! Where do I start?" I whispered. Scared frustrated tears skidded down my cheeks. I wiped them away quickly so Jon and Nick didn't see them.

"I am here," said that same still small voice. "Trust Me."

"I know You are here Lord, but the boys are so small I need someone with skin on."

"What about your babysitting co-op?" the gentle voice said.

I'd figured I'd better start reaching out to the moms in 'Special Care' (my Christian moms' babysitting co-op). *Maybe one of them has an idea* I thought. Using the co-op for our regular daycare routine was out of the question, since I would never have enough free time to fulfill my commitment caring for the other moms' kids. Quieting my concerns, I started making calls.

"Well, you're my second call," I said to my friend Amy. "Do you have any idea where I might find a safe family daycare for my sons?"

"You know my aunt has a neat family daycare. It could be a great situation for the boys. I'll give you her number." Amy began rustling with papers on the other end of the phone call.

"Wow, I can't thank you enough—I'm going to call her right now," I said, my voice breaking a bit with gratitude. I hung up and dialed the number.

A kind voice answered the phone, "This is Ruth speaking."

"Hi my name is Elizabeth Phillips and I am a friend of Amy's," I started with hope. "I'm looking for daycare for my two sons while I work part-time.."

"Oh, I am sorry," she said in a kind voice dashing my hopes with her tone. "I am only looking for full-time kids right now, since I have several part-timers already. I can't take more than eight children."

"I understand," I said and ended the call. I was devastated. She seemed so nice and she was Amy's aunt, which was such a blessing. Ruth had seemed like an answer to prayer. *I believe God will provide someone. But when?* I wondered.

Oh well, back to the co-op list, I thought, close to tears again.

The phone rang startling me. "Hello?" I said.

"Elizabeth, this is Amy. I just spoke to my aunt and told her your situation," she said. "She said she would be happy to care for Nick and Jon. Please call her back and let her know when you need to start.

"Oh, thank you so much!" I said almost squealing with happiness. "I can't tell you how much this means to me." Ruth *was* the answer to my prayer.

We met later that afternoon and the boys took to her right away.

"May we start tomorrow?" I asked her. She nodded and the boys danced with delight. In the morning, I drove over to Ruth's home feeling a little insecure since I didn't know her and I was leaving my sons there. The initial meeting was wonderful but the relationship was still quite new. Ruth greeted us at the door and said "Don't worry Mom, we'll be fine."

Easier said than done.

The day passed somehow. My mind jumped all over the place as I did my work and thought about how things were going at daycare. Soon enough my shift was over and it was time to go get my sons from Ruth's.

Her tidy house looked well-kept and her flower garden was beautiful. I was still on pins and needles as I parked the car. *I wonder how their first day went?* I thought. *I hope everything went well.* I walked up to Ruth's front door which was decorated with a pretty summer wreath. I was so nervous this morning, I didn't notice all of the nice details about her house.

She opened the door and all I saw were smiles. I almost sagged with relief.

"Hi Guys! I'm so glad to see you! Did you have fun?" I asked, giving each of them a big hug.

"M-m-Mommy M-m-Miss Ruth is really nice! Look at all the books she has!" Jon was so enthusiastic I almost giggled.

I looked over at Nick who had returned to his building project. "What do you think Nick?" He looked at me with his biggest smile. I wanted to jump for joy at seeing my sons so happy. I smiled back.

"What are these?" I asked, looking down at the colorful half sheets of paper Ruth had just handed to me.

"Oh, those are daily reports I do for each child. I like to give parents a good idea of what has gone on during the day, any problems or information they should have," Ruth replied with a smile.

"This is terrific," I said as I read about Nick's and Jon's lunch, nap, and how well they played with the other kids.

Ruth's home was completely set up around "her kids." She had a playroom outfitted with a short table and chairs for lunches and snacks—and all the toys and books a child could want. Each child was assigned a cubby and towel for naptime and a hook to hang up jackets and such. It was intangible but there was an evident warmth in her place. I thanked God in silent prayer and gathered up the boys to go home.

As time went on, true to her word, there were reports on both Jon and Nick every day they stayed with her. Her daily reports showed a clear timeline of my sons' behavior and it proved to be critical information. She chronicled the emotional ups and downs that followed supervised visitations with their dad. She could always tell when a supervised visit had occurred, just by the behavior and demeanor of the boys.

Ruth was indeed God's provision for us.

My attorney and I had repeatedly tried to suspend the supervised visits with their father for the last six months. The visits supervised by Dr. Perez at his office every other week were not proving therapeutic. Greg refused to discuss any of Jon's or Nick's questions about the abuse. He even went so far as to accuse them of lying. Dr. Perez had said on more than one occasion that the visits with their dad were doing more harm than good.

I could always tell when Greg was in Dr. Perez's office even without seeing him. I felt as though I had walked into thick darkness whenever he was present, like hitting a brick wall on a motorcycle.

Fortunately the sessions with just the boys and Dr. Perez were going very well. There was definite progress toward healing being made by both boys. It made the setbacks of the supervised visits even more frustrating. Ever since that first visit to Dr. Perez, we went out to supper each week after their session. It became a part of their healing experience.

Several weeks after Jon and Nick started staying with Ruth she took me aside when I came to pick up the boys.

"Jon is having some problems with anger and aggression," she said with concern in her eyes. "He told me that he hates his dad because he did bad things. Recently the father figure for a toy family I have, went missing. Jon finally admitted he threw it behind a massive china cabinet so the 'kids in the toy family didn't have to see him anymore.'"

It saddened me to think that at his young age Jon was trying to protect other children. I wondered if that was because he couldn't change his own situation.

"I want you to know," she continued "I am very familiar with sexual abuse of children—my own granddaughter is a victim," she finished.

"I am so sorry," I said, my voice breaking.

"My son has joint custody of his daughter and his ex-wife has all kinds of boyfriends. We believe someone from that group abused my granddaughter sexually on several occasions. The mom is in total denial and my son has been unable to get the visits stopped. But at least now they are supervised," Ruth explained. "Your son Jon is very angry and my granddaughter experienced that too."

I stood there full of shock that someone else had experienced something like the boys' history. It saddened me to my core. *How common is this junk?* I wondered.

She put her hand on my shoulder "It's so hard to help them understand. We are doing our best to help and protect them but the courts tell us what we can and can't do," she said quiet and angry. Inside me my anger was boiling up even more. I felt like a volcano about to erupt.

"It makes me sad and angry that I even must deal with this." I said, feeling a headache coming on. "I confess it is hard to discipline them, but I know they need it. I feel so bad about what has happened to them. But I do expect them to have good behavior when they are here, though," I said trying to sound firm.

"As do I," Ruth agreed. "I will be using 'time-outs' as necessary, if that's alright with you."

"Absolutely. That's fine. And I will speak to Jon and Nick about their behavior when they are here," I said, already trying to think about what I would say to them.

"Don't be too hard on them," she said smiling. "I do appreciate you speaking to them, but I will handle the situations as they arise."

Little did I know that Jon's "anger episodes" would get much worse before they got better, evolving into full-blown, out of control rages.

"You are a godsend Ruth," I said, with sincere gratitude.

CHAPTER 11

W*HAT A GORGEOUS day!* I thought as the boys, now aged three and four, and I drove west on the highway. *That sky is incredible. It looks like sapphires.* I checked them in their car seats in my rear-view mirror. The boys were still sleeping. This was going to be an amazing day.

I hoped.

I just never knew how they would react to things.

I hope they like the caverns, I mused. It might be a little dark in there for them though, even with the display lighting.

I remembered the previous summer when we went out after dark in the mountains so I could show them the "extra" stars we don't see in the city—*what a disaster!* They didn't care about stars or anything else. They were terrified of the dark and the big pine trees lining the road. Jon and Nick tried to hide, scrunching down in their car seats, and they cried horrible, terror-ridden tears, even though we never left the car. It was so bad; I turned the car around and headed back to the relative safety of the little cabin I rented for our trip. They weren't comfortable until we had all the lights on, door locked, windows checked, and were curled up together on one of the bunk beds.

Oh well, I thought, *they were younger then.*

"I really hope they can see the beauty in the rock formations today," I said to myself, remembering how impressive they had been when I had first seen them several years before.

"Hey Guys, wake up!" I called out. "There are buffalo in that field over there!"

ANTAGONISM AND IRRITATION conferred as they watched. They wanted the best way to get rid of 'that pesky mother' so they could get those little sacrifices for their master.

"We must be subtle and crafty," Antagonism said to Irritation. "We don't want any more headaches, especially in court."

Irritation piped up and said "What about a lightning storm? We could zap her. That would get rid of her, *and* show our master's power!"

Antagonism considered this idea. About to reject it out of hand, he thought of the charred remains of that meddling female and almost chuckled aloud.

He swung around, unable to resist the urge to terrify the underling. Irritation flinched, to the satisfaction of Antagonism.

"All right," he hissed, "but you do it yourself. And you better not screw up—don't touch the prey!"

Irritation scuttled away trying to bow and run at the same time.

"Wow LOOK HOW b...big b...buffalo are!" Jon exclaimed.

"Are they as big as a cow?" asked Nick, remembering a trip to the fair. His memory often astonished me as that visit was seven months ago. But more than that, his clear, melodic voice was a miracle every time he used it. He never even used "baby talk." Just went from "charades" to full sentences. Both boys were doing better with communication. Their therapy with Dr. Perez really seemed to be helping them.

"Actually they are even bigger than the cows and bulls we saw," I replied.

Nick said with fear in his voice, "That is really big. They won't come over to the car will they?"

"No they are only interested in eating the grass," I assured him.

"Are we almost there?" Jon asked. I was glad they had slept most of the way.

"Just about."

I chuckled, having seen the sign that said the turn-off was one mile ahead. "Here we are, guys!" I said as I pulled the car into the gravel parking lot.

"Is EVERYTHING PREPARED?" Antagonism demanded. "We will need a human to scoop up the prey after we immolate the mother."

"Preparations are complete; one of our worshipers is standing by," Irritation muttered. He was beginning to wonder if his foolproof plan was going to work.

Antagonism didn't notice Irritation's doubt. "I can hardly wait to get that prey for the master." He rubbed his hands together in excitement "Death and destruction!" he gloated.

A LIGHT RAIN started as we parked the car.

"Put your hoods up guys," I said as we prepared to make the short hike to the entrance. Jon and Nick, holding tight to my hands on either side, were quiet as we hurried toward the entrance.

BOOM!

BOOM!

The thunder cracked like gunshots!

I thought to myself, *That's pretty close; we better hurry!*

Pulling the boys close I said "Let's get inside guys!"

Suddenly, lightning was flashing all around us with terrifying thunder—shaking the ground under our feet. Now I was frightened too.

"Jesus, cover us with Your wings and protect us!" I cried out.

Even as I yelled into the teeth of the storm, I wondered where that statement came from. *The lightning is right on top of us.*

Running as fast as we could on the shaking irregular ground, I had a mental picture of giant wings covering us from the sky. The wings were deflecting the lightning bolts. Thunder shook the ground with ferocious punches as we finally made it to the entrance of the cave complex. We slipped through the door, skidding with our wet shoes on the linoleum.

Jon and Nick are so scared I thought. *I need to overcome my own fear so I can comfort them.*

Kneeling down, I held them both close and said, "Jesus protected and saved us." As I squeezed them close I told them He would always be with us, watching over us.

It took a long moment, but we all finally stopped shaking and joined the tour. It was quiet and peaceful inside the caverns. Amazing patterns of rock were breathtaking, God-made art to look at. Colors of the rocks ranged from marble white, to orange, to red, and brown. Formed by water dripping minerals down, the timeless cave displays were accented by artistic lighting and soft instrumental music. We headed down the tour path bordered by rope "fences," listening as the guide told us the names of the special areas. God's creation was so beautiful.

"Wow! Look Guys!" I observed as we finished our tour, "The sun is out and the clouds are gone!" I was puzzled by the rapid change in the weather and a little reluctant to leave the safety of the building, but there was no reason not to go to the car.

"Thank You so much Lord for protecting us," I whispered while Nick and Jon discussed what they had seen. To my relief, their fascination with the rock formations had pushed the fear from their minds. There was nothing but excitement in them.

ANTAGONISM GNASHED HIS teeth in anger and frustration. He backhanded Irritation across the dank space.

"What happened? It didn't work! She lives!" he screamed.

Irritation backed away in abject fear, though he knew full well escape was impossible.

"You...you saw and heard what happened," Irritation said miserably." She called on our Great Enemy for protection and He gave it." He knew his response would not improve his situation.

He was doomed.

Antagonism glared at him. At once his eyes flashed and Irritation disappeared in a dark explosion.

A guttural growl captured Antagonism's attention as he dispatched his underling. Antagonism's superior, Violence, had appeared on the scene. When Antagonism felt his presence, he turned to him, cowering.

"I am displeased," Violence growled.

Antagonism, screaming in torment, went into oblivion with his subjugate.

CHAPTER 12

JIM AND I pulled into the courthouse parking lot. As many of the hearings as we had been to, I just couldn't seem to shake that fearful, nauseous feeling in my stomach every time I knew I must see Greg. *What am I afraid of?* I thought.

"Are you doing okay?" Jim asked, stifling a yawn.

"I'm fine, but I'm sorry you're not getting much rest when these hearings are so close together. Your work is busy, too," I said, putting my hand on his shoulder.

"Don't worry, I'm doing fine," he replied. "Didn't you say your counselor would be joining us today?"

"Yes, she'll be here. And her gift of discernment and prayers are powerful!" I said. "Oh, there she is—Hi Grace!"

I was so happy to see her smiling face, I almost ran to her. She was, as usual, dressed in a simple, professional cream blouse, and navy skirt. Her soft brown hair, cut in a bob, highlighted her blue eyes. It was a striking combination.

"Grace, this is my brother, Jim," I said.

"I'm delighted to meet you," Grace said, shaking Jim's hand. "Elizabeth has told me what a wonderful help you and Brenda have been to her." Grace looked around. "Is Brenda watching the boys today? I'd like to have met her as well."

"Yes, she is at Elizabeth's house, and the boys are having fun with my kids," Jim replied.

"Brenda is on call," I said, "with outfits for the boys laid out and ready to go. If the judge demands to see them, she will bring them to court. So far, they haven't had to appear, thank God, and I hope that's the case today."

Jim and Grace both nodded their agreement.

"Let's pray, shall we?" Grace asked. We joined hands, and she started right in. I had to smile even as I bowed my head.

"Gracious Father, we love You and praise You. We give you thanks for Your Presence here with us today. We ask for Your protection around each person, and each family represented here today. Please give the judge wisdom and insight for each situation. We pray for Your will to be done today. We send confusion into the enemy camp! We know our battle is not against flesh and blood. It is against the rulers, against the authorities, against the world powers of this dark world and the spiritual forces of evil. And we thank You, Lord, in advance, for what You will do today. In Jesus' Name, we pray, Amen."

Bolstered, we went inside the courthouse.

Tall and well-dressed in dark gray and black, my attorney, Zachary Taylor, greeted all of us with a ready smile and a kind, "Good Morning."

Zach looked every inch the successful attorney. His single-breasted suit was well-tailored and appeared expensive. His shoes reflected the court lights and somehow made him look intimidating. But his eyes and smile made me feel he was approachable.

I was so thankful for God's provision of Zach. The first attorney I retained never showed up to the first hearing—she didn't even call. Zach was amazing! He always returned my calls the day I left a message for him. He was extremely sharp about family court issues, and his presentation in the courtroom was superb.

I felt very positive about what would happen today, especially since I knew Grace would continue in silent prayer throughout the proceedings.

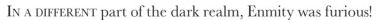

IN A DIFFERENT part of the dark realm, Enmity was furious!

"You are worthless!" he said, kicking and punching toward the face of Dread, newly arrived on the scene. "Your assignment was to keep that counselor away from the hearing. The courts have been a place of strength for us until your idiocy!" Enmity continued, angrily. "Now, those people trying to protect those boys are standing around smiling!"

Enmity continued his tirade, but he was so frustrated; he could hardly speak. Some of his words came out in sputters. This made Dread want to laugh, but he managed to smother all but a little chuckle.

It was still enough to set Enmity off again. He started toward Dread, violence bright in his eyes.

Dread pulled himself up to full stature. At an invisible, inaudible signal, he was surrounded by underlings. Angst, Trepidation, Cowardice, and others. They wouldn't protect Dread, but they would diffuse some of the ferocity of Enmity's attack.

Just before Enmity unleashed his fury, the room exploded in a hazy, blinding light.

"Ouch! @#^@*! Ow! *##*^! No! %$@#!" howls of pain and profanity erupted from the demons around him.

What is going on? thought Enmity. A sharp pain shot up one of his stumpy legs, causing him to stumble. He looked around hoping not to see any of his superior officers. None were around to see this ludicrous mess.

He was lucky.

The underlings held various body parts, screaming out in pain. Dust and soot flew into the air as all the demons jumped and ran around, trying to escape. The chaos made it extraordinarily difficult to see across their filthy cavern. There was confusion everywhere.

Demons injured demons in a frenzy. This was nothing unusual, but it was not of their own choosing. Dread was puzzled until a blast of pain shot from one of his wingtips to the other.

Then he knew.

That rotten counselor was praying again, asking their Enemy to fight them.

As if on cue, all around the cavern were lightning-robed angels of God slashing with their swords. Enmity was again howling in pain, rolling around on the ground. He was as useless as his underlings. Dread was unable to organize his troops or flee from an impending attack. His demon battalion was being slaughtered left and right.

TURNING MY HEAD at just the wrong moment, I caught a glimpse of Greg arriving with his attorney. The only word that came to mind when I saw his lawyer was 'sleazy'.

My sons' father wore an all-too-familiar arrogant smirk as he looked at me. Then his attorney said something obviously sharp, trying to get his attention to tell him something. They 'camped' in their usual location at the opposite end of the hall.

My attorney walked toward Greg's and they met halfway down the hall. Zach smiled at him with an outstretched hand. My ex-husband's attorney shook the proffered hand, though he seemed to hesitate as they met. They had a conversation out of earshot before each attorney returned to his own 'side' of the hall.

"He wants unsupervised visitation again," Zach said with disgust. "Don't worry," he said, reassuring me, "he won't get it."

"The supervised visitation with Dr. Perez is damaging enough," I said. "Even in a therapeutic setting, Greg won't admit anything or answer the boys' questions. So, the visits are disruptive and cause them a lot of stress and emotional turmoil."

"I'll tell them, 'No way!'" Zach said.

Back they both went to the middle of the hall. Discussion ensued. Zach returned, saying, "They want his mom to supervise the visits."

"Right," I said with a heavy dose of sarcasm—then more seriously, "if they ever get the boys in an unsupervised situation, we'll never see them again. Tell them my answer is NO," I said. My voice brooked no argument. I think Greg might have heard me.

"That's what I thought you'd say," he replied with a tiny wink only I could see.

Back at the center of the hall, the attorneys went again, their footsteps echoing in the stone hall. More conversation ensued.

Grace put her hand on my arm. "Don't panic, it will all be okay," she said, smiling.

"I sure hope so," I replied.

"Your attorney is coming back," Grace observed.

"Okay," he began, "they are asking for a professional other than Dr. Perez to supervise some visits. We may have to give a little on this one," he said with the wisdom of experience. "How about if we go through Children's Hospital? I know they have a program and your ex-husband can't really object to that," Zach said.

"All right, if we have to," I said, feeling unsettled and a little concerned.

Back to the center of the hall, the attorneys went again. The two attorneys were attempting to talk, but I could see out of the corner of my eye Greg was with them.. He was gesticulating and being disruptive, until his attorney convinced him to go sit down.

Zach finally returned and said, "I think we may have an agreement. It's time to go see the judge."

The first few hearings had been a shock to me. They were nothing like on TV or in the movies. We never saw the judge until an agreement was reached. I looked around and, as usual, the boys' *guardian ad litem* (supposedly their attorney, protecting their interests) was nowhere to be found. I was exceptionally glad that I had taken my attorney's counsel to plead *nolo contendere*. It meant I did not wish to dispute that something had happened to the boys, but that I wasn't guilty.

Zach was convinced that my appearance and comportment in court would reveal to the judges of the family court what had happened. Because of my plea, I was still considered a part of the case, and as such, my attorney and I were included in all the proceedings. I was glad God arranged that since there was no one else looking out for my sons. I couldn't even remember what their guardian ad litem looked like, having only met him once, very briefly. On the other hand, he wasn't here taking Greg's side either.

"Here we go," my attorney said, opening the door to the courtroom.

Let Your will be done, Lord, I prayed in my head.

Grace, Jim, Zach, and I filed in. I took my 'usual' seat on the right side of the courtroom with my attorney. My brother sat in the 'spectator' area behind me, but I was puzzled by Grace's choice of a seat–in the area behind Greg and his attorney. I realized that not only would she be praying silently, but I could see her smile to encourage me.

Presiding over the case was a different judge than we had seen before. "Do I understand that these children have not seen their father?" the judge asked, with a note of angry concern in his voice.

My attorney stood right away, was recognized by the judge, and said, "The minor children have seen their father every other week for the last nine months, your honor.

My ex-husband's attorney jumped up, evidently thinking he had an opening. "He has only had supervised visitation at their therapist's office," he sputtered a bit.

My 'job' through all of this was to appear calm, somewhat concerned, and composed; in other words, like a 'normal' person.

It was the performance of my life.

My ex-husband tried to get his attorney's attention. When Greg did not immediately receive it, he jumped up and said, "She's crazy, your Honor."

His attorney turned , trying to calm him and get him to sit back down. "She thinks they have been abused in a satanic group—can you believe that?" he said, trying a small laugh.

The courtroom was dead silent.

The judge looked surprised and started flipping through our rather voluminous case file. He looked at my ex-husband, as did everyone else, including the court reporter. "I see no complaint alleging satanic abuse," the judge said. "Do you have something you'd like to share?" the judge asked, almost daring him to answer.

His attorney quickly said, "No, your Honor," before my ex-husband could say anything else. The attorney glared at him as he sat down.

I can't believe what Greg just did to his own case, I thought, shocked. I was so thankful we had kept the complaint confined to sexual and physical abuse. People have a difficult time believing that satanic abuse exists. Even the boys had only told me about the sexual abuse until they were sure I believed them. The satanic nature of the abuse came out a little at a time in bits and pieces, several months after the physical and sexual abuse were accepted facts.

I looked over at Greg, and he looked absolutely petrified in fear. *I've never seen him so scared,* I thought. *Not of me, surely?* I reasoned. *Doesn't the devil support and help those who worship him? I know Satan doesn't love his congregation the way God loves His children, but they are doing his evil bidding. I must remember to ask Grace what she discerned about that,* I decided.

Meanwhile, the judge continued to read through the documents in our case file.

"Mr. Phillips, I see several recommendations from reputable professionals that you are not to be in any unsupervised situation with your sons. How are we going to resolve this?" the judge asked. His tone was severe. He meant business, and he was going to get the answers he was looking for.

His attorney jumped to his feet, "Your Honor, we would suggest that the supervised visits be held at Children's Hospital.

My attorney stood quietly until he was recognized by the judge. "Mrs. Phillips has agreed to an evaluation by the appropriate staff at Children's Hospital for Mr. Phillips and the two young children.

The judge sat a long moment, thinking.

Greg's attorney interrupted the judge's thoughts and said, "Mr. Phillips wants all the supervised visits to be somewhere other than the boys' therapist's office."

"Why is that, Mr. Phillips?" the judge inquired. "You want your sons in therapy, do you not?" he asked Greg, looking at him.

"Well yes, I guess so, but—" he started to say.

"Fine," the judge said, cutting him off. "We will leave the previously ordered supervised visits, and I will also order an evaluation at Children's Hospital for the boys *and* their dad—at least two visits. Is that clear to everyone?" The judge's gaze moved through everyone in the courtroom like a laser.

"Yes, Your Honor," I said, keeping my tone respectful. Greg appeared to be arguing with his attorney. *What is the commotion on the other side of the courtroom?* I wondered to myself.

"Is there a problem, Mr. Phillips?" the judge asked.

"No, Your Honor, we understand," his attorney spoke up, blocking a rising statement from Greg. His lawyer once again stared him into silence, then turned back to the judge.

A sense of movement in the front of the courtroom caught the corner of my eye. First I thought it was a humongous butterfly passing just beyond my vision. *No, can't be,* I thought. *Too cold for that.*

I looked toward the ceiling near the front corner of the courtroom. I didn't see anything, but I felt a presence. I had the same sense about the front corner on the other side, to the left of the judge's seat. I tried to focus, but I didn't see anything there either.

Suddenly I was filled with peace and what I can only describe as humor—like silent laughter.

Could it be possible? I wondered. I had a sense that there were invisible angels in the front corners of the courtroom, and they were laughing. *Do angels laugh?* I wondered to myself. They were seriously scary from what I knew in the Bible, "Fear not" and all that stuff. *A definite puzzle,* I mused.

Jim was holding my coat to help me put it on because everyone was gathering their things to leave. I took another look at the front of the courtroom. I still couldn't see anything, so I turned around to leave. The judge was gone, Zach had an appointment soon, and the clerk was picking up papers. Jim, Grace, and I walked in silence until we were outside the courthouse.

I had to walk by Greg as I passed through the courtroom doors. He appeared to be angry and terrified at the same time. *Why is he so desperate to get the boys alone?* I wondered to myself. I was more convinced than ever. *If he ever succeeds, we will never see them again,* I thought, shivering a little.

"Grace, why did the boys' dad look so scared? Doesn't the devil take care of his own?" I asked.

"No, I don't think so. In fact, I'm sure that for every moment of power or sexual gratification the devil gives people, there are many more times of abject fear." Grace replied.

"Did you see anything in the front of the courtroom toward the end of the hearing?" I asked.

Grace smiled and said, "Why? What did you see?"

"It sounds kind of weird to me, and I didn't physically see anything, but I had the distinct impression that there were angels there. Two angels. Laughing. There was one in each upper corner at the front of the courtroom."

"I'm sure you did," Grace responded, smiling as she got into her car. "See you next week."

This court battle was over for the day. When the realization hit, suddenly I felt worn out. *Jim must be really tired. And now he has to drive all the way back to his house, drop off Brenda and the girls, then go to work.*

"Jim, thank you so much for coming. I'm sorry you have to go back to work," I told him.

"I think I'll go home for a while. I have a meeting tonight," he said.

"I don't know what I would do without you and Brenda."

I was beginning to realize the case took an emotional toll on him as well.

"No problem," he said.

Jim and I got in his car and headed back to my house. "Looks like God protected the boys once again," I said. "I am so thankful."

CHAPTER 13

UPSTAIRS, DOING DISHES, I heard furious screams and ripping paper sounds coming from the basement.

Oh my gosh! What in the world?

I worriedly dried my hands and threw down the dish towel. As I headed for the basement stairs, I looked around, spotting Nick. He was calm, coloring with Susan's children at the coffee table. I flew down the steps two at a time, praying I didn't fall on the way. The screams of rage continued as my stomach twisted in knots. *Something is radically wrong–maybe evil?* My palms were so sweaty and clammy they almost slipped on the banister.

As I entered Chuck's and Susan's basement, I saw Jon standing in full rage. He was in the middle of the bedroom he shared with Nick, screaming in infuriation like I had never heard him. Clutched in his fists were scraps of paper. His face was beet-red as he shook with wrath. I had to admit, I was a little afraid. *Afraid of my own child?.*

Susan came down to check on the commotion. She took one look at Jon, and then at me. With concern in her eyes, she turned around and went back upstairs to care for the other kids.

I pulled myself up straight and walked over to Jon, saying, "Honey, what's wrong?"

His eyes were unfocused, cloudy. Without a word, he took a wild swing at me with his small fist.

He was trying to hit me!

Shocked and unsure what else to do, I picked him up from the behind in a hug, pinning his arms at his sides. He continued screaming, angrier than ever. I was surprised at his strength. He began kicking his legs now, totally out of control of his emotions. I held on to him with some effort but managed to sit down on the bed. I crossed one of my legs over both of his. He was wholly pinned down in this way, and it seemed to increase his rage–if that was even possible. I was totally at a loss, and my heart stung my chest as it broke for him. He had never behaved in this way before, not even close. It was like he was a different person. It was like someone put a cloak of crazed fury on my little one, and he was suffocating in it.

I realized then that the evil I felt wasn't emanating from Jon. It was, in fact, separate, and somewhere in the room.

"THAT'S DELICIOUS!" SAID Tantrum to Rage with a fiendish grin.

"Totally out of control," agreed Rage.

"That woman will surely give up now," Tantrum continued. "Did you see him try to hit her?"

"I don't know–she's surprised us before," Rage cautioned, "but that was pretty funny.."

"This is the first of many episodes like this I have planned," Tantrum said, eyes glittering in the dim light. "That mother will tire of it. Her pride in her parenting skills will be damaged. She will abandon him emotionally, though I suspect she may continue to care for his physical needs. And that guilt will also work to our advantage. We will be the ones to obtain these boys for the master and he will reward us," Tantrum enthused.

"You'd better be right!" Rage warned.

"IT'S OKAY, JON. You're all right. You are going to be okay," I kept saying, in what I hoped was a soothing tone. While talking to Jon, I prayed silently for help and guidance. Tears erupted from my heart and escaped my eyes, running down my cheeks.

All at once, I felt his body relax and he began to cry. *Whew*, I thought. *I'm so glad that's over.*

The sense of evil went away.

What happened?

I released his legs and softened my hold on his arms. He turned around to me and I enfolded him in a sincere hug while he cried and sobbed tears that broke the rest of my cracked heart.

As his sobs subsided, I looked him in the eyes (which were now back to normal), and I said, "I love you. You hear me? That will never change." He put his arms around my neck and hugged me again, nodding.

"Honey, what happened to your drawing?" I asked in a soft voice. "You and Dr. Perez worked on that, right?"

The drawing was a tracing of the outline of Jon's fully clothed body on a massive piece of paper. Jon colored it in-- hair, clothes, even shoes. He was quite proud to bring it home when he and Dr. Perez finished working with it.

"Dr. Perez said it showed that I was strong, but I still have to see Dad," Jon said in a tortured voice. "He makes me so mad, but I am not strong enough to beat him up," he finished, sounding defeated.

"Is that what you want to do?" I asked him.

"Yeah, I wanna rip him apart," Jon said, still furious but no longer out of control.

Oh wow, now what do I do?

That still, small voice in my head said, "Don't do or say anything. Just love him."

With impeccable timing, Susan called down the stairs, "Who wants some dessert?"

Jon looked at me, at the mess of crumpled, ripped paper, and then back at me. I smiled and said, "We'll clean that up later. Let's go get some dessert!" He grinned. "Race you upstairs," I challenged.

I called Dr. Perez the next day.

"Actually, it's good, in a way." Dr. Perez responded when I told him about the events of the previous evening. "We don't want him to keep all that anger bottled up inside," he said.

"They both seem to have so much trouble after the supervised visits," I said. But I've never seen anything like this. Can't we get the supervised visits stopped at least for a while?" I asked.

"I'm working on that now," Dr. Perez began. "I've written a report with my findings regarding the negative effects of the supervised visits. And that was before your experience last night. The boys' father will not discuss and certainly not admit that there has been any abuse of these children. His response, the few times the boys have brought it up, is to say they are lying. This is very unhealthy for them. They know what happened. The person who was there with them is saying it didn't happen. It is a setback for them every time."

I sighed but listened.

"Lately," he continued, "the boys' father has been pressuring me for the original videotape of one of their sessions that was particularly disturbing. He says he is going to get a court order, so he can have it," Dr. Perez said, a wary note in his voice.

I was alarmed. "If Greg ever gets the original, he'll find a way to destroy it and claim that any copies have been edited or altered."

"I won't give the tape to him regardless of how he threatens me– or my staff," Dr. Perez said firmly. "I have told Wendy that when he calls, if he is in the least impolite, never mind abusive, to her on the phone, she is to put the call through to me. I don't even want her to have to deal with him."

"I wish I could say I'm surprised at his behavior," I said. "But I am sorry that he is putting you through this. We have another hearing coming up soon. If you could share your concerns about the effects of the supervised visits, maybe the court will stop them for a while, at least," I suggested.

And that is precisely what happened.

Greg and his attorney were furious at the judge's ruling in the next hearing. But Dr. Perez's report figured into the judge's decision and he suspended the supervised visits for an indefinite length of time.

Thank you so much Jesus!

Jon had a few more fits of rage, but they were less intense. Eventually, they went away as the supervised visits were suspended. Both Nick and Jon were happier and more relaxed when they became convinced that their dad wouldn't be in their session every other week. I often prayed that the supervised visits wouldn't be resumed.

Bedtimes were also more manageable.

One evening we were reading a book given to the boys by Susan. It was very colorful and all about a circus parade. Jon and Nick really enjoyed it. They were dozing off as I reached the end of the book. The last page of the book held a quotation from Jeremiah 29:11. The page seemed lit from within. It said, "For I know the plans I have for you declares the Lord. Plans to prosper you and not to harm you, plans to give you hope and a future."

This is how the Lord showed me my life verse.

RAGE HELD TANTRUM by the throat.

Tantrum's wings and feet flapped around like dying fish as his hands tried unsuccessfully to keep Rage from choking him. "You said she would give up on those kids. I told everyone we had them in the bag. Now things are even worse. The dad has no chance of getting them alone now," Rage howled. "Somebody must pay for this failure and it's not going to be me!"

Tantrum stopped kicking and fighting, despairing of his depleted existence. Rage threw him across the cavern and stomped off to his own doom. Tantrum lay unmoving on the cavern floor as a horde of minor demons descended on him and gleefully ripped him limb from limb.

CHAPTER 14

ANOTHER TRIP TO *the courthouse,* I thought with a silent, inward groan. At least it wasn't a hearing today, just picking up some paperwork. Jon and Nick were curious about this "court" place I had to go to from time to time, asking as I drove.

"Will Dad be there today, Mommy?" Jon asked with trepidation in his voice.

"I don't think so," I said, shooting up a mental prayer to God that would keep him away.

No matter how hard I tried to conceal it, they could always tell I was stressed at best and upset at worst after a visit to "court." But despite the possibility of seeing their father, the boys were excited about going to get a burger after our visit to the courthouse.

I told them as we were entering, "Guys, I need you to be on your best, quietest behavior. This is a grown-up place and people are busy working." Fortunately, through God's grace and our efforts, Nick and Jon had not been required to appear in court. Part of me wondered if my ex-husband didn't want to risk what they might say if they were there.

Jon was dressed, in his usual t-shirt and shorts but Nick, was in full cowboy regalia. He wore his hat, a vest made by my mom, a red, black, and white bandana, boots, and chaps. His toy six-gun was in its holster cinched by a belt. Those days, he dressed like a cowboy virtually all the time. He liked nothing better than to ride his bouncy horse in full cowboy splendor.

I did not think anything about his attire as we went into the courthouse. I walked through the metal detector first, then turned and watched as Jon passed through without incident. Nick was a different story.

The burly sheriff's deputy stopped Nick before he entered the metal detector and demanded that he hand over his beloved toy cowboy revolver. Nick started to get angry, and I began feeling anxious in the pit of my stomach. The deputy became wary and I rushed back through the metal detector to Nick's side.

Dumb, I mentally chided myself. *Why didn't I have the foresight to have him leave the gun in the car and just wear the belt and holster to go inside?* It never occurred to me that anyone would consider a cheap toy to be a threat. *All I needed at this juncture in the boys' case was to be arrested for trying to sneak a gun into the courthouse!*

Intervening, I assured Nick that he would get his toy back when we were ready to leave.

"Isn't that right, Deputy," I asked, using my "mom-eye" so he would know this was a serious issue.

The deputy replied in a flat tone, "We confiscate all weapons entering the building, ma'am."

I turned to Nick, who was hanging on to his gun in its holster for dear life. I knelt, so he could look into my eyes and see my solemn, severe expression. I didn't want him to think he was in trouble, but I did want him to know this was a very big deal.

"Nick, this officer has a job to do," I said. "He protects the people who come to court, including us. You need to let him see your gun." Nick reluctantly handed it over, business end first. It looked like he was pointing it at the deputy. The deputy took the toy and placed it in a drawer behind him. Nick started to cry, and the tears were huge as they poured down his stricken face.

"Honey, we'll get your gun when we are ready to leave. Now we need to pick up the papers that Mommy needs," I said, in a no-nonsense voice. I stood up and proceeded forward. We all passed through the metal detector without a problem this time. I found the appropriate office and retrieved the paperwork I needed. As we headed back down the hall toward the entrance, I began praying that the deputy would find it in his heart to return Nick's toy.

I stopped at the security desk and said, "May we please have my son's toy back? I apologize, and I promise it won't happen again," I said.

The deputy looked at me and then at Nick's tear-stained face. "I guess a cowboy needs a six-gun," he said in all seriousness. "I am not supposed to return confiscated items, but since it is an obviously important toy, I will this time." I was thrilled–another prayer answered.

The officer retrieved the toy from the drawer and explained to Nick, "You need to learn to handle a gun properly. If you hand it to someone, point it down and give them the butt to hold onto. If an officer ever asks you to see it, do it right away, Okay?"

Jon began snickering and said, "Mommy, he said, 'butt'."

"Yes, he did. That's what you call the handle of a gun," I said, stifling a chuckle at Jon's reaction. The last thing I wanted to do was antagonize the deputy who had finally warmed up a little.

Nick had his toy back in its holster, I had my papers, and we left before anything else could happen. As we walked to the car, I spoke quietly to Nick. "When we go somewhere like this or church or other grown-up places, we need to leave your gun in the car.

"Okay, Mommy." His hand kept hold of the gun, and his eyes were still very big.

THE DISCOMFORT IN the cavern was almost palpable. Low-level functionaries glanced about with nervous expressions while fingering the crystals hung about their necks as if the crystals could save them. Those further up in the hierarchy stood discussing some contentious subject. There was never any real agreement, just lesser or greater wrangling.

"You cannot possibly believe those sinful, guilt-wracked humans and their prayers can have any effect on our abilities, do you?" sneered Arrogance. "They are so unaware of our Enemy's true purpose and love for them; they may as well be running around in the dark."

Arrogance always answered his own questions. To everyone's surprise, Pride said, "I tend to agree but you aren't the first one to notice."

Selfishness snarled, "So what *is* the problem then? We have not been able to get those boys even remotely close to capture!" Selfishness turned to Accident and Illness, pointing a sooty, boney finger at them. "You two have not done your jobs on that female or anyone she cares about."

Together, Accident and Illness said, "It…it should have worked!" They started babbling, overlapping their excuses with shrill voices. "We are prevented and stymied at every turn…There is always a great battle being waged by her, her people, and the Enemy's agents assigned to protect her…We are unable to assail her!"

"She is so ignorant! She knows nothing of the battle against us. What are you talking about?" Selfishness glared at them.

They whined, almost in unison, "The Enemy is teaching her, and she has wise humans helping her."

Selfishness growled, "What about the car wreck that should have killed her when you caused her to fall asleep while driving? It was a risky plan; the boys might have been damaged. But with her dead, at least then the boys' father would have had free rein to offer them to our master."

Selfishness, screaming with frustration, yelled, "But it didn't work, now did it?!" Pulling aside the veil to reveal some of the physical realm, he said, "Listen to how she describes the incident to her friend."

"Lisa, you aren't even going to believe what happened the other night," I confided over a cup of tea. "I was driving the boys over to see Perry Johnson. He's the detective investigating our case. Anyway, he wanted to see us, and the only appointment he had available after I got off work was at 5:30 pm, right in the middle of rush hour. So, after work that day, I picked the boys up from Ruth's home and we went to meet with Detective Johnson."

My thoughts drifted back to that night as I related the story to my friend.

Wow! It is so cold! I thought. *I have to turn up the car heater.* "Are you two warm enough back there?" I asked the boys.

"Yeah, Mommy," came the stereo reply from the backseat.

"Did you take your hats and mittens off already?"

"Yeah, we did," replied Jon.

"Did you throw them on the floor?" I asked, knowing the answer already.

"Yup, Mommy, they're down there," Nick said as he leaned forward in his car seat to verify the location of their cold-weather gear.

"What happens if you get cold?" I asked.

"You'll turn up the car heater, right, Mommy?" Jon said.

I had to chuckle. "Yes, you're right. But next time, put your stuff on the seat between your car seats, so you can reach it if you need it, okay?"

"Okay. Can we have our sandwiches now?"

"How did you know we have sandwiches?" I asked.

"We saw Miss Ruth give them to you," Jon snickered, thinking he had "put something over" on Mom.

"Well, you are right. I'll get them for you. It was nice of Miss

Ruth to do that for us. Be sure and thank her tomorrow, okay?" I said.

"OK, Mommy, we will," Jon replied.

"Can we have some Christmas music, please?" Nick requested.

"Sure, I'll put a cassette in the tape player," I replied. My sons and I simply love Christmas music. I was happy to oblige.

All settled, I said, "Here we go."

I saw the traffic on the westbound freeway was a little heavy but not too bad for 5:00 pm on a weeknight. I looked down at my speedometer–55 miles per hour. No need to rush, we had plenty of time to get to our appointment. My exit was coming up; *I'd better stay right here in the far-right lane, so I can get off soon,* I thought.

"Elizabeth, wake up!" a man's deep voice said. "Elizabeth Anne, it's time to wake up *now!*" His tone was all firmness but not unkind.

My eyes popped open.

I was going 65 miles per hour in the far-left lane.

The fast lane.

There were cars all around mine. *Where is my exit? Where am I? How did I get across four lanes of bumper to bumper rush hour traffic?* Thoughts jumbled through my brain. I glanced down at the clock—5:15!

Fifteen minutes had passed.

I've got to get off this freeway, I thought with rising panic as my hands and arms began to shake. *How could this be? Was I really asleep for 15 minutes? I hadn't felt sleepy; I was actually looking forward to hearing what Perry was going to tell me about his investigation. I am miles beyond the exit I was supposed to take...what happened?*

Oh, here's an exit, I thought as I made my way off the freeway. We were a long way from where we were supposed to be. *How did I not hit someone or something?*

By God's grace, no one hit us as I was moving across four lanes of heavy rush hour traffic. *No one even honked at me.* I got off the freeway, found a parking space and sat in my seat shaking from head to toe. I started praying and thanking God that He had protected my sons, me, and everyone in the traffic around us. I investigated the backseat to see Jon and Nick peacefully sleeping.

Lisa's eyes were wide as saucers, and her mouth was an "O" as she waited for me to finish the story.

My memories of that night continued replaying in my head. Tears rolled down my cheeks as the realization of what could have happened dawned on me. Somehow, someone *had* to have been driving my car. Fifteen minutes was just too long and there were too many opportunities to have collided with someone's car or some object along the freeway.

A thought ran through my mind that perhaps an angel had been dispatched to drive my car and wake me gently. It's amazing I didn't crash when I woke up so disoriented. The still, small voice in my head spoke to me then.

It said, "I have big plans for Jon and Nick."

That made me so happy, renewing His promise to me that He would save them out of this nightmare.

"God is so good!" I said to Lisa.

Shocked, Lisa said, "That is amazing! Praise the Lord for a real miracle! I'm so glad you and the boys are alright," she said, giving me a hug.

SELFISHNESS ALLOWED THE "curtain" between the spiritual and physical realms to drop back into place. He turned on Accident and Illness, both now cowering. He screamed at them, "Your pitiful, ineffectual efforts did nothing but bring glory to our Enemy!" Selfishness said, spitting on the filthy cavern floor. "You two are lucky our master enjoys the effects of your work much of the time elsewhere, or I would banish you both right now!"

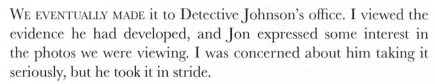

WE EVENTUALLY MADE it to Detective Johnson's office. I viewed the evidence he had developed, and Jon expressed some interest in the photos we were viewing. I was concerned about him taking it seriously, but he took it in stride.

He looked at the photo line-up with great care and spent some time looking at each photo. All except the last two, a man and a woman. His body language revealed his evident anxiety and I told him he had done a great job.

As we left to go home, unbeknownst to Jon and Nick, Detective Johnson slipped a piece of paper into my coat pocket.

I remembered the note after the boys went to bed. The message chilled me to the bone when I read, "The photos Jon reacted to are people of interest in this case. Have you thought about hiding the boys or going 'underground'?"

CHAPTER 15

VISITING MY COLLEGE roommate and her husband at their home had been a welcome respite from "the case," as I had been referring to it lately.

"Emily, I can't thank you and Larry enough for this evening!" I told them. "A chance to relax and not think about horrible things for a change."

"We are so glad to see you! You and the boys seem to be doing well," Emily replied.

"It's a battle. But tonight was amazing!" I said. "I have been having so much fun, I totally lost track of time. I'd better get the boys ready for bed. They often fall asleep in the car and it is so much easier when I can just pop them into bed once I get home."

I went into the guest bathroom with the diaper bag, holding Nick's hand.

"C'mon Buddy, let's get you ready for sleepy time," I told him. He laid down on the floor in front of where I was kneeling. "Good job," I told him, smiling. "Now let's change the diaper," I said after removing his chaps, cowboy vest, pants, and t-shirt.

"Mommy, did you know Sara has a penis?" Nick asked me, as if this was a normal topic of conversation.

I had to shove my shock down and keep a straight face. It was physically painful to do.

There had been no recent revelations, no reports of issues from

Ruth at daycare, and no discussion amongst the three of us about the case. Both boys were calm and happy, now that the supervised visitation had been stopped permanently, I hoped. Not sure exactly how to respond, I finished his diaper and plastic pants and said, "I thought you guys said Sara wears dresses."

"She does. But she has a penis," Nick said in a matter of fact tone.

My heart began aching. "How do you know that?" I asked. *Watch it Elizabeth,* I inwardly chided myself for the all too direct question. I didn't want to make him think I didn't believe what he was telling me.

"Well, she took it out and peed on my tummy," Nick replied. "I really didn't like that," he said with a scrunched-up face.

"I'm not surprised. That doesn't sound like a nice thing to do at all," I said, trying to sound supportive while inside, my anger was a volcano about to erupt. "Here comes your pajama top," I said as normally as I could manage.

"Yeah, and Dad was mad because he said now he had to wash our clothes before we came home," Nick said. As Nick said that, I remembered an incident that had puzzled me at the time.

When he dropped off the boys, Greg handed me their little suitcase and said, "I did their laundry," with a peculiar expression on his face. I thanked him, and he left. I was puzzled because he had not done that before or since. I wondered at the time if perhaps he was trying to share in their care a little more, but now I was beginning to understand. And something occurred to me.

I asked Nick, "Honey, you said Sara peed on you, right? Was it yellow, kind of like water?"

"No, it was white and icky," Nick answered with the scrunched-up expression on his face again.

My heart went into my shoes. I felt like I threw up a little bit in my mouth. There was no way a three-year-old should know about semen.

"Honey, I am so sorry she did that. It was wrong," I said, patting his head. Nick was shutting down; I could see it. His eyes seemed to say that he felt he had said too much. I desperately wanted to ask him more questions, but I held back. I had learned, finally, asking more questions now would only make him reluctant to talk about his experiences in the future.

Finished with diapers, footed pajamas and blanket sleeper, I hoisted him into the air, tickling him a bit. He giggled, and I said, "Go get your brother please, it's his turn."

As I got Jon ready for bed, I had to practically bite my tongue to keep from asking him about Nick's revelation. But I knew better than to betray Nick's confidence. I had no idea if Jon was even present for the incident. I didn't want to be accused by the court of 'coaching' the boys, so I kept our conversation light and general.

With reluctance, we said good-bye to Emily and Larry. The boys were quiet on the way home. When I looked back and saw them, sound asleep in their car seats, I had to smile.

After an abbreviated hug and kiss good night, Jon and Nick were soon asleep in their beds. Even though I was shaken to the core and very tired, I knew I needed to put the details in my growing file of what my attorney called 'contemporaneous notes.' They needed to be recorded at the time of an event or revelation.

I wrote in detail what Nick had told me. *Why was Sara of 'Matt and Sara' referred to by the boys as a girl who wore dresses?* I ruminated. *How old was this person, obviously a post-pubescent male? Was it actually Matt dressing as a female? What possible reason could he have for ejaculating on Nick's stomach?*

Questions rioted in my head. I realized it was just another puzzle piece and I wondered if I would ever figure out what really happened.

CHAPTER 16

AN UNEVENTFUL THURSDAY *afternoon at home*, I thought, *just the way I like it.*
BRRRRING, BRRRRING!

The peace of my afternoon was shattered by the noise. *Why was that phone ringer so loud?* I wondered with irritation. Except for my scheduled calls with my parents, phone calls were virtually never good news.

"Hi, Mrs. Phillips. This is Perry Johnson calling," the voice said.

I relaxed a bit and said, "Hi Perry! How are you?"

"Just fine; nothing has changed. I just have something I'd like to run by you."

"Okay, what is it?" I wasn't sure whether to be alarmed or intrigued.

"What would you think about taking the boys for a ride around the neighborhood to see if they respond at all to any particular locations?"

"I am always glad to do whatever I can to help you with your case, but I don't want to put any more pressure on my boys if we can help it."

"I don't want that either, so I thought we could just say that we are going for a ride in my patrol vehicle. I could let them turn on the lights and show them how things work. It should be kind of fun for them."

"Okay, that sounds fine. When would you like to go?"

"Are you available this coming Saturday morning?"

"Yeah, as a matter of fact, I am off this weekend. I won't tell the guys much; just that we are going to see you and you can explain the rest when we get there, would that be alright?"

"That sounds fine, I'll see you at 10:00 am?"

"We'll be there."

"Do you understand your assignment, or are you too stupid?" Vexation spoke rudely, as he always did, to Peevishness.

"Yes, milord," Peevishness replied with heavy sarcasm. "I am to blind the eyes of the boys, their ridiculous mother, and that meddling detective to any of our locals' habitations. Is that it?" Peevishness said in mock earnestness.

"Just see that you do it. Or else," Vexation threatened.

Slightly cowed by the threat of his superior, Peevishness said, "Okay, okay, I've got it."

Opening the curtains in the bedroom, I took in the bright sunshine and said with a smile, "Hey Guys, time to get up!"

Jon was the first to sit up. Returning my smile he asked, "Is today the day we're going to see Detective Johnson?"

I glanced over to the other crib across the room where Nick was slowly waking up. "Yes, it is. Let's get ready and have some breakfast so we can go."

A shadow seemed to cross Jon's and Nick's faces almost simultaneously. "Dad won't be there, will he?" Jon asked with temerity.

Surprised, I responded, "No, I don't think so. We're going to see Detective Johnson. I don't suppose your dad would want to see him, do you?"

Both boys answered, "Nope, I don't think so," looking at each other with slight, conspiratorial smiles.

"Mommy?" Nick said.

"Yeah, Honey, what is it?" I said, thanking God again for his speech.

"Can we have pancakes?"

"Absolutely, that's a great idea!" I said, removing him from the crib. After completing his diaper change, I pointed to his outfit for the day "Put your clothes on, please? I laid them out over there." I turned to Jon, who had neatly set down his clothes. "Good job with your sleeper and pajamas, Jon. Do you want to try the potty?" I asked.

"Yeah," Jon responded.

"Yea! Good job! Let's put on your training pants so you can get dressed, and I can start the pancakes."

I'm so glad I asked everyone to pray for the outing, I thought, hoping today would be a good day.

Animated, the boys discussed the upcoming visit to the police station as we drove. *It's so great to hear them talking like little boys,* I thought as I drove.

"Mommy, will we be able to pick up Detective Johnson's gun?" Nick. While it was his favorite outfit, today he wasn't dressed as a cowboy. His toy six gun was at home, put away.

"I kind of doubt it, but you'll have to ask him," I said, musing on a boy's fascination with guns for a moment.. "Okay; now Guys, remember what we talked about how we behave in the police station. There are people busy working, so we need to be quiet, right?" I asked as we pulled into the parking lot.

"Inside voices, right, Mommy?" Jon said, looking pleased with himself.

"That's right, and be sure to stay with me," I reminded them.

"If there is something you want to look at, we need to ask Detective Johnson."

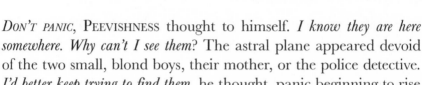

Don't panic, Peevishness thought to himself. *I know they are here somewhere. Why can't I see them?* The astral plane appeared devoid of the two small, blond boys, their mother, or the police detective. *I'd better keep trying to find them*, he thought, panic beginning to rise in him again. *How can I blind them if I can't locate them to begin with?* There were many bubbles of impaired vision on the astral plane today–some large, some smaller–where those hated Christians were praying to protect someone or something from view.

Maybe they are in one of those bubbles, Peevishness thought with dread.

He had heard that the mother had been prompted to pray that 'their home would be invisible'. There was no way she could understand the true depth of *why*. She'd still be wondering about it, if Joseph hadn't explained the secret of the master's forces projecting themselves on to the astral plane.

Joseph was one of those brats at the Street High School for homeless kids. His parents had kicked him out, understandably, when he turned to Christ after being raised to worship the master. Peev couldn't understand why the mother volunteered there, when she had troubles of her own. Nevertheless, the mother's prayers were being answered. No one had been able to locate the place in which the boys were living, even after much concerted effort among the master's servants.

Suddenly, Peevishness remembered his assignment and Vexation's threat. Vexation would surely banish him if he couldn't complete his assignment, and the prey gave any more information to the other side.

Foreboding stood by, laughing at Peevishness and his predicament. A thought crossed his mind ever so briefly.

He could help Peevishness?

Oh, no way, this is my favorite form of entertainment, he thought with a fiendish grin.

I GUESS THERE aren't many people working today, I thought, but the guys are doing a good job anyway. Climbing the massive staircase, with its black linoleum and many layers of paint on the handrail, I held the hand of each son. I was glad we didn't have to use the grimy banister. Indeed, the stairs were indented from footsteps over the years. The indentations were in the center of each stair, not near the sides.

I spotted Detective Perry Johnson across a huge room full of desks and work areas. Next to a desk piled with papers, he was on the phone with his back to us. His hands were moving around in animated conversation. Although he appeared angry from the back, I could not hear what he was saying. I stopped at the top of the stairs and looked around, trying to find a subtle way to announce our presence to him. Suddenly, I heard footsteps on the stairs behind us. Another detective came up the stairs and said, "May I help you?"

I smiled and said, "Yes, please. We're here to see Detective Johnson," glad to be out of the awkward spot I'd found myself in.

"Just a sec," he said and strode across the large open room. He spoke to Detective Johnson, and I saw 'our' detective turn towards us and smile. The other detective came back and said, "He'll be done in just a minute." Looking down at Jon and Nick, he said, "Have fun!" with a smile and went on his way.

A minute or so later, Detective Johnson waved us over to his desk. "I'm sorry to keep you waiting–a slight emergency," he said with a smile.

"If this is a bad time, we can…"

"No, no. This is a good time," he assured me, grinning at the boys. Focusing on Nick and Jon, Detective Johnson said, "How're you guys today?" He shook each of their proffered hands. I smiled at their manners.

Nick looked up at me and asked, "Can I ask him now?"

"Sure, Honey, you can ask," I said, muffling a chuckle. Detective Johnson looked from him to me and back to him, puzzled.

Nick started to ask but seemed to lose his nerve. Jon broke in and said, "He wants to know if he can see your gun." Then he stepped back with a satisfied look on his face. Nick nodded; his eyes very big.

To his credit, Detective Johnson was all business as he replied, "I will show it to you if you promise me some things."

"What?" both boys said in unison.

He looked them each in the eye in turn and solemnly said, "Promise me that you will never touch, pick up, or try to use any gun until you are over eighteen, have taken a gun safety class, and have talked to me first."

Since, by this time, I had one boy sitting on each knee so my face was behind them , I smiled and nodded my appreciation to Perry.

"Jon, do you promise?"

Jon's eyes were large and serious as he looked at me, and then answered, "I promise." Perry then looked at Nick and said, "Nick, do you promise?" Nick paused, seeming a little perplexed, but said, "Yeah, I promise. But what about Dad?"

"What about your dad?" Detective Johnson asked with gentleness in his voice.

"Well, he has a gun…" Nick started to say, but Jon broke in again and said, "Yeah, a shotgun."

I knew about the shotgun. Greg had it when we were still married, but Perry was now on high alert.

"We touched it because he showed it to us and said we could, but we didn't pick it up," Nick said in a mournful tone, certain that his chance to see the detective's gun was now gone.

"Alright. But from now on, you both promise, right?" Detective Johnson said in all seriousness.

"We promise," they said in unison, looking relieved.

"Just a minute," Detective Johnson said as he retrieved his service revolver from a locked drawer in his desk. He turned a little away from us and checked the chamber and the safety. Satisfied that the gun would not fire in its current state, he turned back around and carefully placed it on the desk pointed away from himself and all of us.

"You know that this is not a toy gun, right?" he asked the guys. They both nodded, their eyes as big as saucers. "This is a .38 caliber pistol, and I only use it to protect myself or someone who might be hurt if I didn't use it. It is not like on TV. If I have to use it, it could badly hurt or kill someone," he intoned.

"We know," Jon said. "The policeman at Dad's friend's house shot someone in the leg," Jon continued.

"Then they cut his neck off," Nick said quietly.

Cut his neck off? What in the world does that mean?

"Honey, what do you mean by "cut his neck off?" I asked in a quiet voice.

Nick's response was to draw his index finger across his neck.

Cut his head off? Was it possible that they saw a beheading? I'm afraid I might throw up. I wanted to scream and escape this whole thing, but there was nowhere to go. He was obviously describing what he had seen. An adult would say something like cutting someone's head off or removing someone's head. But Nick was describing where the cut was made. Why? Was this a sacrifice?

I tried unsuccessfully to catch Perry's eye to warn him not to react, but he was already composing himself. "Wow, that must have been scary," the detective said.

"Yeah, and the gun was really loud!" Jon said.

"Did it look like this gun or more like your Dad's?" Perry asked, working hard to avoid leading their responses.

"It wasn't like Dad's. The gun was like yours…but smaller, I think," Jon said.

"Did the policeman dress in a suit like me or some other way?" the detective inquired.

"He wore all dark blue with a badge and a hat and a big belt," Nick explained.

"Was the policeman always there when you were there?" Perry asked cautiously.

"Yeah, most of the time. Especially when the doctor was there," Jon confided.

"Did the doctor have a uniform?" Perry asked.

"Not like the policeman. His was green with lots of pockets," Jon said. "The doctor was there when they took the babies out of the moms' stomachs," Jon whispered.

I had a strong suspicion about the fate of those babies.

As usual, I was unprepared for these revelations. I couldn't believe I was surprised again. *Most of our life together as a family was so normal, except for weekly counseling and the occasional visit to court. The jarring times dealing with the horror the boys had experienced always left me feeling shaky and in shock,* I thought, shuddering a bit.

"Who wants to go for a ride in my police car?" Perry asked with a big smile and a wink. I thanked God silently for Perry's redirection.

He slipped his service weapon into a shoulder holster under his jacket. We all stood up, and Perry and I exchanged glances over the boys' heads as they got into their jackets.

We will talk later, his look said.

We walked to the parking lot, and both guys wanted to hold Detective Johnson's hands. He seemed pleased with that and cautioned them about stepping off the curb without looking both ways.

FOREBODING HAD GONE from chuckling at Peev's predicament to outright laughter. He couldn't see any way for Peevishness to complete his assignment, and he knew Vexation would not be kind or quick about Peevishness' punishment. "Delicious!" Foreboding guffawed, rubbing his filthy, misshapen hands together in glee.

Using mental power, he reached a chill hand into Peevishness' chest and squeezed his heart. *Careful,'* he thought to himself, *it wouldn't do to obliterate Vexation's protégé before Vex was able to do it himself. Besides, watching a banishment was almost as good as doing one himself.* Foreboding grinned to himself.

As the chill spread from his heart through his body, Peevishness moved his mind away from accomplishing the assignment to finding a way to avoid banishment to the abyss.

No one has been able to penetrate those bubbles of protection, he rationalized. He knew Vexation would ask how long the protection had been in place, but Peevishness didn't know. He had considered the assignment beneath his talents, so he had not attached himself to the subjects in the astral plane right away. Perhaps there was something else in play here. *Our Enemy?* he thought.

"No, I don't think so," Peev said aloud. "Why would the Highest God get involved with such small fry?"

Anyway, Peev would have had plenty of time if those Christians hadn't gotten in the way. Even that pathetic mother was learning to do battle on a spiritual level. *Who was teaching her?* he wondered.

One thing he knew. Once a devoted Christian learned about spiritual warfare, it made their lives miserable.

Not that the hierarchy would accept any excuses.

CHAPTER 17

PERRY LED THE way to his vehicle, a souped-up, four-wheel-drive SUV. Just as he opened the back passenger door, I realized that the boys' car seats were still in my car. "Detective Johnson, the guys' car seats are still in my back seat. Should I go get them?" I asked.

"Your car is out front, right?"

"Yes, they know they have to ride in them. I'd like to get them and get the boys strapped in before we take off."

"Let's do this," he replied. "Since you can't drive your car into the backlot with the police vehicles, I'm going to show the boys the special things in my car. Then, we'll strap them into seatbelts just long enough to drive around to the front lot, where we can put their car seats in my car for our ride, Okay?"

"Sounds fine." Perry was a cop, and the drive was short, but I still had the feeling it was not precisely legal.

Perry was already showing them the radio and scanner. After they were done looking, Detective Johnson called the dispatcher on the radio to tell her he was leaving the station in his vehicle. "10-4, be careful out there," she responded, much to the boys' delight. He showed them the big, red light he used for emergencies, and since it was on the floor, he let them each turn it on and then off. It was very bright, and they almost shook with excitement at being given permission to touch it at all, let alone turn it on.

Perry drove, very safely, around to the front lot where I retrieved their seats, and installed them. I told them they needed to be in their car seats as usual. "And besides," I said with great intellect, "you can see better sitting up higher."

They liked my logic and climbed into their seats like experts. I strapped them in and gave them a final check by giving each belt a good tug. *All secure,* I thought and climbed into the front seat.

As we drove out of the lot, suddenly, Jon said, "Detective Johnson, have you ever been to Dixie's restaurant?"

He looked a little surprised and answered, "Yes, I have. My kids like to go there. Have you been there?"

Nick responded, "Yeah, our Dad takes us there sometimes."

"Do you like Dixie's?" asked Detective Johnson.

This time Jon responded, "Yeah, but we don't like our Dad."

I was not included in any of the conversation at this point. Perry had told me on the phone that I should sit in front and observe the boys but not say or do anything that might influence their reactions as he drove. His plan was to drive around the neighborhoods near a home where illegal activity was suspected. As we drove past Dixie's restaurant, the boys animatedly pointed it out to Detective Johnson. I considered taking them there for lunch after our 'outing'.

Perry made a gradual circle of the neighborhoods around Dixie's restaurant. Since their father lived near there, the detective made it a point to avoid venturing too near Greg's apartment complex. I appreciated him avoiding that location. I didn't want that reaction of familiarity from Nick and Jon since they had been there so many times.

Every now and again, in a casual turn around, I'd check on them. I noticed they seemed increasingly uncomfortable every time we began to head south. I turned back to the front, and we traveled several more blocks in the same direction.

All of a sudden, I heard a sharp, scared cry from the backseat. It felt like someone yanked a large, somewhat dull butcher knife from my chest to my throat. I turned in my seat just in time to see both boys struggling to slide down out of their car seats toward the floor. They were trying to get as low as possible. I glanced out the windshield, shocked to see a stylized, Tudor style townhouse with what looked like a thatched roof.

It had an olive green upper story, chocolate brown on the ground level, and was detailed in thick black trim all around. The appearance of a "thatched roof" came from tan roof shingles. The building was the spitting image of a small ceramic magnet the boys had a strong reaction to at a friend's house. She took it off the refrigerator immediately and later gave it to me. It would have been a pretty house, but for the boys' terror, which colored it with a filmy charcoal overlay of their fear. The magnet was a very accurate representation, and that scared me too, now that I'd seen the real house. Reaching in my purse, I felt the magnet, which I'd forgotten to take out. I snatched my fingers away as if it had bitten me.

Jon and Nick were becoming more frantic by the minute. Tugging at their car seat straps and crying out of fear or anger, I couldn't tell whether they were afraid, or angry, or both.

"PERRY, GET US OUT OF HERE!" I shouted, leaning into the back seat as far as my now loosened seatbelt would allow. I put one hand on each boy's knee.

Detective Johnson complied with my terrified request, making a sharp right turn and speeding down the next block. Then, at a more moderate speed, we returned to the police station.

Once we parked at the police station, I climbed into the backseat between the boys' car seats. The boys had shed a few tears but seemed better now that we were away from that house. The look of abject terror and betrayal in their eyes seared my heart. I think they thought we were taking them back there.. As I tried to console them, a couple of tears escaped my eyes. When Perry suggested this 'ride' I had not expected any real reactions from them because they were so young. How could I be so very wrong? The only upside was that we had gained some valuable information.

Was it worth it? I wondered.

I could tell Perry felt badly too.

We all went into the station, and Perry showed us what I had come to think of as a 'forensic' playroom. The room was full of lots of toys, and the distraction worked wonders for the boys. They had, unfortunately, become very familiar with similar playrooms having had several different professional evaluations. The various people we had worked with handled our situation so well that now the boys' reaction to these playrooms was curiosity about what toys and books they held. As long as they could see me through a window, they were content to explore the room.

"Okay, Guys. I'm going to talk with Detective Johnson for a few minutes, okay?" I said it matter-of-factly, though I was thoroughly shaken inside. Closing the door, the detective's mask of professionalism slipped to show his concern and sorrow.

"First of all," Perry started, "let me say that I'm sorry the ride upset the boys so much. That was unexpected, and not my intention at all," Perry said apologetically.

"I agreed to it. And I wasn't expecting anything to happen either. Were you able to get the address of that location?" I asked as I reached into my purse.

"Oh, yes, I got it!" he said. He looked shocked when I pulled the magnet out of my purse and handed it to him. I was glad to be rid of that horrible thing.

"May I make a copy of this?"

"Sure. You can keep it if you want," I said, looking over. I smiled, waving to the guys. They returned to industrious play.

"Why don't you hold on to it, and I'll request it later if I need to. Be right back." I was almost sad to have to keep the thing.

When Perry returned from the copier, he said, "I will find out what I can about the occupants of that house. Addresses and driver's licenses are part of the public record. In the meantime, you should prepare yourself and the boys to go 'underground'." As he spoke, his eyes filled with sadness.

I must have looked shocked because he added, "As a law

enforcement officer, I can't help you officially. But if you need a name to get started, be sure to let me know," he said emphatically.

Underground, I thought, dismayed. That was a huge step, almost irretrievable.

I had seen it in the news. Moms traveled with their children, person to person, house to house, across the country to escape abusive fathers and uncaring court systems. The secretive process was loosely fashioned after the "underground railroad" utilized by slaves escaping to freedom in the previous century. Members of the modern network welcomed moms and kids into safe houses. They supplied them with clothing, documents, and even cars sometimes.

When the courts failed to protect children, 'going underground' was a solution of last resort.

The Federal Bureau of Investigation was actively pursuing some of these women and members of the network. *It's easier than catching criminals,* I guessed. Some moms sent their children to loved ones, going to jail rather than revealing the children's location to the courts, and abusive fathers. Going underground often meant never again being in contact with friends and family. But it must have been worth it, to protect the mothers as well as the children being sheltered.

I would do anything to keep Jon and Nick safe! I thought.

If I had to go underground, having Perry's referral would ease the way. Members of the networks had to be very careful and sure of the people they were helping. There was a small percentage of people who had no grounds to keep their children away from the other parent. But so many more needed help because they were in truly desperate situations. I had to admit, if my ex-husband or his family and friends ever had the boys in an unsupervised situation, I don't think I would ever see my sons again.

We were essentially 'in hiding' already And I was extremely careful. But the thought of uprooting, leaving everything behind and never seeing my family and friends again was daunting. Here was an experienced detective telling me it may be necessary. *I'm not sure I can handle this*, I thought, panicking.

A Bible verse came to mind, and I spoke it quietly to myself. "I can do all things through Christ who strengthens me." (Philippians 4:13) I mentally thanked God for the comforting reminder.

"Are you all right?" Perry asked, concerned.

"Ah, yeah…yes, I think so. I'll do some serious thinking about what you said," I mumbled. I composed myself, and we went over to the playroom.

"Wow!" I said with a smile. "Looks like you guys have been having fun."

"Look, Mommy, look at my train!" Nick said, proudly showing me a track set-up, he had made.

"That's terrific!"

I looked over at my other little one. "How are you doing, Jon?"

He was sitting in a small nook with a book and seemed a little troubled. I desperately hoped he hadn't resumed thinking I knew about the abuse while it was occurring. Putting aside the book he had been looking at, he said, "Okay, I guess."

I wasn't sure what to say, so I told him, "Let's put the books and toys away, please, so we can get some lunch."

Perry pitched in and helped us with the clean-up. While he was helping, he said to Nick and Jon, "Thank you both for coming to see me today. If there is ever anything you want me to know, ask your mom to call me, and I'll be happy to listen. Got it?"

We all shook hands and left for lunch. I had decided against Dixie's.

At lunch, Nick, Jon, and I had a great time, but soon both guys were sleepy. They went down for their naps quickly when we got home. I spent their naptime thinking about new identities for all three of us.

The still, small voice in my mind said, "*You can do all this planning if it makes you feel better, but you will not have to go underground.*"

I remembered a verse I had read earlier that week which struck me, so I looked it up in my journal. It was Proverbs 10:30. "The righteous will never be uprooted.,"

Was this a promise to me? I wondered.

Not fully certain, I thought it might be good to make some preliminary plans. I hoped God would not be upset with me about that.

CHAPTER 18

"DID YOU TWO have a good talk with Dr. Perez?" I asked as we walked to the car.

"Yeah," Jon said. "Nick just wanted to play with the cowboys and covered wagon, but I talked to Dr. Perez.

"That's great, Hon. Did you have fun, Nick?" I asked.

"Yeah, it was okay. But Jon kicked over my wagon."

"Jon, why did you kick over his wagon?" I asked, stopping to look at him.

"I don't know. But Dr. Perez said there are better ways to show my anger. I colored a whole page with black. He said that was a good way. After I finished, we threw it away."

Jon was very angry sometimes, now that he felt safe enough to express it. On rare occasions, he even tried to hurt his brother. It worried me, but Dr. Perez said that it was a normal response to what he had been through. Though adult intervention was necessary, the boys were nearly the same size and strength. I had to continue to hope and pray that it was unlikely Jon would actually injure Nick. I felt a chill inside to think of one of my beloved sons injuring the other.

"Did you apologize to Nick?" I asked.

He turned to his brother. "I'm sorry, Nick," Jon said earnestly.

"Nick, can you forgive Jon?" I requested.

"Well yeah," he said. "But don't do it again."

"Okay, I won't," Jon promised.

"Good job, Guys!" Changing the subject, I asked, "Where would you like to have supper tonight?"

"Dixie's!" they said, almost in unison.

"Are you sure?" I had to admit, I was a little taken aback at their enthusiasm.

"Yeah, yeah! That's where we want to go!"

I was still a bit puzzled but I said, "Okay with me," as I finished buckling them up. After all, this was a whole different city and restaurant than the one they had identified for Detective Johnson. We had never been to Dixie's, at least, not together. If I had been thinking about it, I might have suggested a different restaurant, so Dixie's would remain exclusive to their experience with their father. I wish they had chosen another. Did God have plans for our evening meal? A divine appointment of sorts? I did tell them they could make the choice of restaurant on counseling nights.

I guess we were going to Dixie's.

Snow crunched and squeaked underfoot as we crossed the parking lot. *Wow, it's cold tonight!* I thought to myself. *It must be really cold for the snow to squeak.*

The hostess seated us in the restaurant with me facing the door. I always felt a need to be vigilant and protective of the boys, so I usually sat so I could see who came in. I wanted to be alert if their dad or his family came in. The boys clambered into their booster seats at our booth, looking for the expected crayons and coloring pages.

"What would you like to eat?" I asked.

"Mac and cheese; it's delicious here," Jon said in a grown-up way that surprised me.

"Okay," I said, chuckling at Jon's grown-up comment.

His choice didn't surprise me. It was always a favorite for him. I ate macaroni and cheese for lunch almost every day I was pregnant with Jon. It was my only craving.

While looking at the menu, I asked, "Nick, what would you like?"

Receiving no response, I looked up at him. His eyes were huge, terrified saucers, and he was staring at someone in horror. My stomach dropped to my knees.

I looked at Jon.

His reaction was the same as his brother's.

I tried to be casual as I looked in their direction. I saw an older man with long, stringy hair come through the door. He didn't notice us, as he was too busy shaking off the cold and snow. With worn, dirty clothes, he looked to be in his fifties and had a face that showed he'd led a hard life. I hadn't thought much about it since unusual characters were common in this college town. I leaned in and whispered across the table, "Guys, what's wrong?"

Nick continued to stare, and Jon whispered back, "That's Matt," (of 'Matt and Sara').

Despite the booster seats, they both were trying to scrunch down to make themselves less visible. I felt shattered by an electric shock running through my body. The boys were scared and so was I. Was this one of the people who had abused them?

Had Holy Spirit brought us here? I wondered. That thought was followed by silent but desperate prayer. *Please protect us Lord!*

My mind raced, full of jumbled thoughts.. *Should I call Perry Johnson? This is probably out of his jurisdiction. I can't call the local police.* The man had done nothing suspicious while in the restaurant. *What if the boys were mistaken? What to do?*

Meanwhile, Nick and Jon tried unsuccessfully to hide under the table. Wiggling and whimpering as they were, they were inadvertently calling more attention to us. *Not good!*

"Guys sit up in your seats right now," I whispered with urgency in my voice. They obeyed, but the terror was still with them.

'Matt' was seated somewhere behind me, so I had to turn

completely around to see him. I couldn't keep turning around to look. *That's so obvious.*

Recalling a scene from an old movie, I removed a little mirror from my purse and surreptitiously gazed at the man Jon and Nick called Matt. He was looking at his menu. So far, the man had not had any discernible reaction to the boys' presence.

"Hi, I'm Candy, I'll be your server tonight," the teenager by the table said. I almost jumped.

Dinner, I thought, *I almost forgot.* I was almost shaken out of my desperate thoughts, realizing she wanted to take our orders. *'Should we stay or go? The boys need to eat supper and we're almost an hour from home. I didn't want to disappoint them since we always ate supper out on counseling nights. It was something they looked forward to.*

The still, small voice rested a calm, quiet thought on my racing brain.

Get it to-go.

Of course, that's what I'll do, I thought, smiling up at her.

"We need this 'to-go' please?" I said.

"Okay, what would you like?" Candy asked, a little puzzled, but trying to hide it.

"Jon, what would you like to have?" I asked.

"Mac and cheese, please," Jon responded. His voice trembled, but I smiled and nodded my approval of his good manners as he gave his order.

"Nick, how about you?" I inquired.

"I would like chicken fingers, please," Nick told our server. I smiled at him and at the momentary distraction from his staring at Matt.

"And for you, ma'am?" the pert, little server asked.

"Nothing for me. Thank you," I said, in keeping with my budgeting efforts. Besides, at this age, the boys usually had some leftovers from their orders. The thought crossed my mind, *'Do I look old enough to be called, ma'am?* That thought ran away as another quiet suggestion came to me.

See if you can get the license plate number on his car.

Now I could see the reason for getting our food 'to-go.' *That's it. The boys can eat their supper in our car, and we can wait until Matt comes out and gets in his.* Doubts assailed me. *What if he walked to the restaurant even though it was so cold? What if I miss him, or can't get the license number quickly enough?* These thoughts were interrupted by the arrival of our food. It smelled delicious! I almost wished I'd ordered something.

After leaving a nice tip for Candy, we put on jackets and hurried to the cash register.

Matt had left his seat and was now at the counter, nursing a cup of coffee. We had to pass by him. There was no other way to get to the exit.

Jon and Nick folded themselves into my coat to hide their faces as we passed by. He noticed the boys. There was nothing I could say or do but hurriedly pay my check. As he looked at them, something akin to surprised fear showed in his eyes. I felt chilled by something dark and foreign when I happened to catch his gaze, and it made me shiver a bit inside my jacket. Realizing I had been holding my breath the whole time, I practically threw the money at the server and rushed the boys out of the restaurant and into the cold.

Arriving back at our car, I had the boys get into their car seats. Once fastened in, I gave them each their supper. They were hungry and tore into their food. I was thankful they did not mention the encounter in the restaurant. I almost began to wonder if they were mistaken but with a heightened sense of apprehension, I looked around the small parking lot.

I moved my car to what I thought might be a good vantage point. Fortunately, the lot was well lit. *How can I keep track of the cars?* I wondered.

Another quiet thought entered my mind, *'Maybe I could make a grid.*

I wrote down all the license plate numbers I could see (and the state if they were from another state). It took a moment, but soon all the cars and trucks were in their relative positions on my paper. There were two I just couldn't see well enough. *Should I chance getting out to get a better look? What if Matt came out while I was out of the car?* My thoughts wanted to start racing again. *Well,* I told myself, *I'm not going to follow him. So, I'm in the parking lot, what can he say?*

Nick and Jon were strenuous in their objections to the idea of me leaving the relative safety of the car. But I reassured them and asked them to watch the restaurant door for me. I left the car engine running so they would stay warm and told them to eat their food.

I was as fast as I could be in the cold night and with relative ease, I got the two numbers I needed. Triumphant, I jumped back in the car and locked all the doors, shivering from cold and fear. I turned the car off, hoping to remain hidden.

Now we wait for this 'Matt' person to come out, I told myself. *This is not a fancy restaurant, he should be out soon,* I hoped, looking at my gas gauge. I was glad I had just filled the gas tank. I needed to turn on the car periodically to keep us from freezing in the parking lot.

"Guys," I said, "are you really, *really* sure he was Matt? Could it be someone who looks like him?" I was unable to stop myself from asking, though I was almost certain I saw recognition in his eyes when he looked at the boys.

"It was him, Mommy," Jon said with resignation.

"I believe you," I said, in a resolute tone. "I'm glad you are sure. We are going to wait for him to come out, get his license plate number, and then we will give it to Detective Johnson." The boys, somewhat mollified, returned to eating their dinner. They were scared, but they didn't stop eating.

Various patrons came out and left in their vehicles. As they did, I marked them off the rough diagram I made. I wrote down the license plate numbers of new arrivals in case they were there to pick him up.

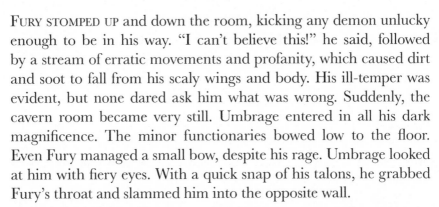

FURY STOMPED UP and down the room, kicking any demon unlucky enough to be in his way. "I can't believe this!" he said, followed by a stream of erratic movements and profanity, which caused dirt and soot to fall from his scaly wings and body. His ill-temper was evident, but none dared ask him what was wrong. Suddenly, the cavern room became very still. Umbrage entered in all his dark magnificence. The minor functionaries bowed low to the floor. Even Fury managed a small bow, despite his rage. Umbrage looked at him with fiery eyes. With a quick snap of his talons, he grabbed Fury's throat and slammed him into the opposite wall.

"Sorry, milord," Fury managed when he regained his breath.

"What is your problem?" Umbrage spat at Fury, kicking a small demon for emphasis.

"The meddlesome woman…" Fury began to say.

Umbrage roared, "*Which* woman? There are too many Christians getting in our way! Every hour, new Christians are involved. Our Enemy is outrageously patient with them, and some are learning to do battle. Which woman do you mean?!"

"The mother of the two young brothers desired by our master… and also her praying people," Fury offered as an answer.

"I do remember hearing something about that situation–total incompetence!" Umbrage sneered.

Fury started to speak again, his anger close to rebellion, "Right now, they are sitting in a car waiting to trap one of our more prolific suppliers."

"And just how did she know how to find him?" Umbrage asked with condescension thick in his voice.

"I can't figure it out," spat Fury in total frustration. "Those boys wanted to go to a particular restaurant," Fury started to explain. "Their mother listens to and believes them even when they say things that should be outrageous and unbelievable to her—"

"So?" Umbrage fired back.

"So," Fury explained, "for some unknown reason, our supplier decided to eat at that particular restaurant tonight. Those brats recognized him. Now the mom is sitting in her car trying to see which car he gets into. Probably so she can give the license plate information to that policeman who is helping them

"You should have dealt with the policeman before now!" Umbrage roared again, his eyes blazing.

Fury was shaken but managed to squeak, "We've tried several times, but he is protected by our Enemy, because of the prayers of the mother and her people.

I'M SO GLAD the boys fell asleep I thought, glancing in the rearview mirror. *The quiet music seems to help but I am getting sleepy too,* I mused. I wiggled my toes trying to warm my feet. *This is crazy. I wonder if I should have given up and gone home. It's way past the boys' bedtime and they were starting to get restless being in their car seats so long. I can't blame them. What can that man be doing in Dixie's for over two hours?* Time crawled by ever so slowly.

Well, since they are asleep and relatively comfortable, I'll wait just a little longer. I hate to give up without getting the information I need. It's getting late and I have to get up for work tomorrow, I worried. I wished I could read, but I couldn't have the lights on in the car.

Two and a half hours, what can he possibly be doing? I wondered if he walked to the restaurant and left by some other entrance. *I'll wait ten more minutes,* I decided, *and then I'll go. Maybe I was mistaken in thinking I was being led to do this,* I thought with weariness.

Suddenly, a motion at the restaurant entrance caught my attention. I sank down in my seat so I would be less visible. I could just barely see over the bottom edge of the car door window.

The man the boys had identified as Matt came through the

entrance doors. He paused, looking around suspiciously. I was scared. I couldn't help but see him as some sort of a monster.

Don't be such a baby, I scolded myself. *He doesn't know we're still here or what kind of car I drive.* He paused and looked around again. His demeanor and behavior made me even more sure of the boys' identification. He was 'Matt.' He was one of their abusers. I suddenly realized that my fingers and toes felt frozen.

Breathe, Elizabeth!

He started walking across the parking lot and I held my breath again, hoping he would get into one of the remaining cars and not just keep walking. He walked over to a vehicle and unlocked the door of one of the cars that had been there the longest. As he pulled out of the lot, I double-checked the license plate number on my paper and put a big circle around it. When he was gone, I breathed a huge sigh of relief. *Finally.* Now, home to bed for me and two sleepy boys.

"Thank You, Lord for your guidance and protection tonight. Please bring us safely home," I prayed quietly, hoping not to wake my sons. I was very satisfied with the information I had obtained.

The next day, I spoke to Perry and gave him the license plate number. He seemed pleased and said, "I can't believe you did a stake-out at the restaurant. Maybe we should offer you a job."

I laughed and said, "I couldn't have done it if it wasn't for my sons. Please let me know what you can about what you find out, O.K.?"

"I will tell you anything I legally can, I promise," he said.

Several weeks later, Detective Johnson called. He requested to see Jon and Nick at our home. I checked with Susan, my housemate, and she agreed.

We arranged a time and Susan decided to take her kids to the park while Detective Johnson was there with us. He brought another photo "line-up" of drivers' license photos for the boys to view. This time it included photos from information developed from the investigation of the house the boys had identified. The man from Dixie's was in the photo lineup as well. Those photos were disturbing to

Nick and Jon, who both started running around the room and refusing to answer any more questions. They had become physically hyperactive, unable to handle their emotions.

Detective Johnson later told me that they had correctly identified the owners of the house in question as well as the man they called 'Matt' from among several random drivers' license photos. Perry said he would put the case together and present it to the Assistant District Attorney. I waited to hear from him, but when I did, the news was not good.

"Mrs. Phillips?" a male voice on the phone said.

"Hi, Perry!" I said when I recognized the voice.

"Hi Elizabeth, I want to let you know what is going on with the case. Unfortunately, the A.D.A. is refusing to prosecute but I'm going to try again. I thought we had a strong case the first time I took it in," he finished with a tinge of sadness in his voice.

"I can't believe that!" I remarked with dismay. "Is there anything I can do? Do you need anything more from me?" I asked.

"No, the evidence stands on its own merits. I don't know what the problem is. It almost seems like there is someone or something interfering with the case. Does your ex-husband know anyone in the D.A.'s office?"

"Not that I'm aware of," I said with anger, "but there is apparently lots of stuff I didn't know about."

"Well, I'll do my best to get her to look at this," Perry said.

"And I will pray."

"That's always appreciated," Perry said.

Is the enemy interfering in the District Attorney's office? Grace did tell me that the enemy does a good job controlling the courts and legal system.

According to Perry, the second try with the A.D.A. went no better than the first. She refused to even review the evidence. Perry's third try was to go over her head to the District Attorney. The D.A. asked the ages of the witnesses and upon discovering they were children, gave him the file right back. He didn't even look at it.

"No way," said the District Attorney. "You and I both know this is just a bitter, vindictive ex-wife trying to cause trouble for her ex-spouse."

As time went on the case eventually went cold and there was no further action on the part of the police. Perry was frustrated, but soon enough, we were out of contact. I was amazed, puzzled, and truly disappointed, but very glad that my hope for our protection was in the Lord, not in the criminal justice system.

CHAPTER 19

"WHAT IS THIS one about?" Jim said, only slightly exasperated as we drove into the courthouse parking lot.

"I know; another day, another hearing," I said, feeling weary of the whole process. "I can't even remember how many this makes," I continued. Evidently, Greg was agitating for unsupervised visitation again. The hearing a few weeks ago went well for us. The judge wanted to study the case and granted a continuance until today.

"Fortunately, the protective order is still in place. Even the supervised visitation was suspended because Greg was trying to intimidate Dr. Perez and wasn't willing to discuss anything the boys brought up," I related as we stepped through the courthouse doors. "Besides, the supervised visitation was doing more damage than good, so Dr. Perez put a stop to it. I don't know what he's up to today."

There was the usual procession of attorneys going back and forth between the two 'camps in the hall.' Walking back and forth, my ex-husband's attorney was pushing hard for unsupervised visitation and I was saying "absolutely not." Unable to come to an agreement in the hall, we went before the judge without anything in place. The judge in Family Court would have to decide.

My counselor, Grace, and I prayed before we walked through the doors. As we did, I felt a sense of peace about the outcome. It rested on me like a hand on my shoulder, bolstering my courage. We trooped into the courtroom and sat as the judge took his seat.

The judge started by making some cursory remarks about the importance of an intact father-son relationship. This made me feel slightly panicky, so I glanced over at Grace. She was continuing to pray and appeared unperturbed.

He continued, "There is ample evidence of a real problem here, and it would be irresponsible to send these children back into a situation which has caused them harm. However, I would like to see these problems resolved. So, I am reinstating the order for supervised visitation with a new evaluator."

My breath caught in my throat while my stomach started doing backflips. All thoughts of peaceful faith went out the window. I noticed Grace still appeared to be praying.

"Elizabeth, we are going to have to agree to at least an evaluation," my attorney told me quietly.

"They have to go through it all again?" I asked, tears threatening though I tried to appear calm.

Before I realized what was happening, my attorney was on his feet, talking to the judge. "We would agree to an evaluation, with subsequently supervised visitation contingent upon the results of that evaluation."

"Does the father have someone in mind to do the evaluation?" the judge asked as he looked toward Greg's lawyers.

Greg's attorney started to object to the evaluation instead of visitation. The judge cast a skeptical eye on his arising objections and said, "Is there someone you could recommend to the court for an evaluation or not?"

There was some verbal scrambling at the other table, and they came up with a name.

"Is this person a psychologist or psychiatrist, or what?" the judge asked with intensity.

"A psychiatrist, Your Honor," said Greg's attorney.

"O.K., I order that the minor children and both parents undergo evaluation by this psychiatrist. There will be at least two supervised visits, unless the psychiatrist cannot make a determination or needs an additional session. This is not an open-ended order for supervised visitation, as I have read the reports of the boys' therapist. He is convinced that more contact with the father would not be therapeutic at this time."

It felt as though huge waves of fury came from the other table, breaking over my attorney and me. I felt overwhelmed with the intimidation, but my attorney didn't seem to notice the anger from the other side.

It seems so unfair to put the boys through that–telling their whole story again. Putting them through the memories, fear and sadness seems like torture to me, I thought. The tears threatened again.

"The mother retains full custody for now. Mrs. Phillips, you will make sure that this evaluation happens, but I want Mr. Phillips to make the arrangements and pay for the sessions," the judge said firmly.

We all stood, and the judge left the bench. I looked for Grace, and she smiled at me. Jim started to say something, but I cut him off and said, "Let's wait until we get outside."

When Jim, Grace, and I reached the car, Jim said, "What just happened there?" I shook my head, afraid to speak, lest my tears escape. On the other side of the parking lot, my ex-husband and his attorney were jubilant. Their happy voices and 'high fives' were hard to watch and hear. Inside, I was so disappointed. I wondered, *has God forgotten my boys?* Intellectually, I knew God loves us and is faithful, but my heart was full of pain. There was nothing to do but go home. Fortunately, I had a few minutes to compose myself, so I didn't frighten the boys.

THE DEMONS DANCED, jumping about in the darkness of the cavern. "Now we'll be able to get those boys for the master!" they shouted.

Umbrage was pleased but not sure this latest decision would bring about the desired result.

A COUPLE OF weeks went by without any contact from Greg. I was still trying to pray but feeling forlorn in my heart.

Then the phone rang one day. When I answered, I heard an unfamiliar male voice. He identified himself as Dr. Findley, the psychiatrist selected by my ex-husband. He asked if the boys and I might be able to come to his office the following Friday. I replied, "Yes, that would be fine." He gave me the details and directions to his office.

I told him, "My ex-husband is ordered by the court to pay you for these sessions. I want to be sure you are paid for your time."

Dr. Findley said, "Thank you for letting me know. That wasn't mentioned by Mr. Phillips, and I will speak to him about it. If you don't hear otherwise, I'll see you and the boys a week from Friday."

The appointed day came all too soon.

I had already explained to Nick and Jon that they would be seeing another therapist.

"Is Dr. Perez OK? Dad didn't hurt him, did he?" Jon said. His voice held some apprehension tinged with anger.

"Dr. Perez is fine. You and Nick will still see him each week," I assured him. Their concerns addressed, Jon and Nick went back to playing quietly, as we had a few minutes before we had to leave for the appointment. I didn't want to get there so early that I might have to deal with Greg without the therapist present. *I am so concerned about this, Lord,* I prayed silently. Then I decided to kneel down by my bed to pray some more.

As hard as I tried not to cry, hot tears escaped my eyelids and slid down my cheeks. Suddenly, I felt a gentle but firm pressure surrounding my whole body. *That feels like a hug,* I thought. The realization dawned on me: *God gave me a real, tangible hug. Now I know everything will be all right.* I wiped the tears off my cheeks and felt myself smiling as I stood up.

"C'mon on Guys! Let's go to your appointment," I said with an almost happy note in my voice.

This latest evaluation was not the victory Greg was hoping for. Dr. Findley reported to the court that there was a definite problem between the boys and their father, and he would not recommend even supervised visitation at this time.

God hadn't deserted us or forgotten us.

In the long run, having this additional professional opinion gave more weight to the case protecting Jon and Nick. It was a little easier for me to trust what God was doing after this, even when the decisions of some of the various hearings seemed to go against us.

CHAPTER 20

TERROR LAUGHED AT the ineptitude of the other demons. *I have the answer to getting rid of that meddling mom,* he thought to himself. *And get those boys for a sacrifice to the master. My specialty will achieve for the master what every other demon has failed to do. And it should be easy.*

I WAS BONE-WEARY from the long day, ready for it to be over. My bed and pillow felt wonderful, waiting for me with a comforting weight of sheets and quilts to keep me warm against the frigid night. I felt secure and drifted off to sleep.

But wait! my mind screamed. *What is going on?*

There was a feeling, like a blackness trying to infiltrate my skin. *Open your eyes or you will die!* I tried to blink, but my eyelids had turned to stone. *Why can't I open my eyes?* I tried to turn on a light, but my arms and legs wouldn't move. I was paralyzed, all the way from toes and fingertips to my eyelids. Like a heavy stone lowered slowly by a crane, a weight came down on my chest, spreading throughout the length of me on the bed. I felt like I was suffocating, crushed under the weight all over my body. I tried to pray for help, but no words came out. My lips wouldn't move. My tongue stuck to the bottom of my jaw. And the weighted blackness was getting deeper and deeper.

I can't breathe! My mind was in full panic mode. *I am going to die. Open your eyes,* my brain implored. *Open your eyes or you will die.*

I can't get them open. I can't see what is crushing me! Are my ribs going to fracture from the pressure? My heart was thudding so hard, it seemed audible. Breaking through the terrified, jumbled thoughts in my brain, came the still, small voice. *"Praise Jesus,"* it said.

I can't get the words out. My voice is paralyzed. What can I do? I'm going to die.

"Start in your mind," the voice in my head said. *"In your spirit."*

I'm not sure this is going to work, but I'll try. Praise You Jesus, He alone is God. Praise, honor and glory to You, Lord, my spirit began to worship. My brain was still in an uproar, but as I continued to praise God in my spirit, I could feel the black weight covering me begin to lighten, ever so slightly.

I was still so scared; I don't know if I'd ever been so terrified. I kept praising God in my spirit, and I was finally able to get my eyes open. *I think I can move my head, not very much though.*

It was painful and shallow, that first breath. But it came. So, did another. Not only that, I felt less afraid. My mind began to assess the situation a bit more clearly. I was still terrified. *But I think someone is fighting for me. As a matter of fact, I am sure of it.*

My breathing deepened and slowed to a more normal rate. At least I didn't feel like I was suffocating anymore. I tried my voice.

"Praise God, He is mighty to save," came out of my mouth.

The blackness began to lift again, clearly affected by my words. "He is my Rock and my Salvation! I will not be afraid," I said. The suffocating blackness finally began to fade away. As I continued to praise the Lord, the force became lighter in color and weight before disappearing completely. I tried to move my feet. Little by little, I began to be able to move my hands too.

I sat up in bed and the heaviness was gone. I went in to check on Jon and Nick. They were sleeping peacefully. Nick's quiet, little snore was reassuring.

I went back to my room and turned on the light. While I was thanking God for saving my life, I realized I was still feeling panicked. *What in the world was that?* I wondered.

It took a while, but once exhausted, I fell asleep with the light on.

The next night, I felt frightened and reluctant to go to my room for the night. *You have to work tomorrow. Go to bed,* I chided myself. I fell asleep without incident. Two nights later, was a different story. After the nights of peaceful sleep, I wasn't prepared for what happened that third night.

The blackness was back.

If possible, it was deeper and more frightening than before. My heart pounded and I was once again unable to move or speak. I started praising God in my spirit again. This time it didn't seem to be working!

Oh no! My breath was weak, ragged, and I felt as though my heart would burst.

"Don't give up," the still, small voice said in my thoughts, *"Keep fighting."*

So, I kept praising God and trying to focus on Him. Soon, I sensed some lifting of the weighty, horrifying darkness. "Thank You God for saving me!" were the first words out of my mouth.

On my next counseling appointment, I asked Grace about the horrific episodes.

"Am I going nuts?"

She was not the least bit mystified. "Those are trances," she explained.

"I thought they might be nightmares, but I have never been paralyzed by a nightmare, nor have I had it continue after I was awake," I said, puzzled.

"Trances are a horrible tool of the enemy," Grace said. "They are designed to terrify you into forgetting to ask God for help. They can settle in as oppression and take up residence in your house. We need to pray and ask God to clean out any remaining oppression in the Name of Jesus. And you need to do it in each room of your house when you get home. Remember, Isaiah 54:17 says, 'No weapon formed against us shall prosper.'" Grace embraced me as she reminded me. "Here's another great one. 2 Timothy 1:7. 'God has not given us a spirit of fear but of power and of love and of sound mind.'"

As Grace had predicted, the attacks continued when I tried to go to bed. I felt fearful for some time. But I had my weapons now, and the trances began to gradually lose some of their power.

First, the presence over me seemed less inky black, then it became greyer, then slightly less heavy and not quite so smothering.

By God's grace, I became able to fight back faster and stronger. It took several months, as my fear became less and less, but the oppression went away altogether. I was once again blessed with 'sweet sleep' (from Proverbs 3:24, "when you lie down, you will not be afraid; when you lie down, your sleep will be sweet").

TERROR NO LONGER laughed. He stood, confronted by three higher-ranking demons. "What's the matter, Terror? Not as easy as you thought?" the demon known as Bestiality taunted.

He shoved Terror into another demon, Pedophilia, who punched him in the area where a human's stomach would be. Terror doubled over in pain. Pedophilia caught his jaw with a vicious uppercut that snapped Terror's neck back, almost removing his head. He staggered back into Slavery, who kicked him.

"The master still wants those boys. What are you going to do about it?"

Terror knew he was doomed.

Arguing only prolonged the inevitable. The three higher-ranking demons closed in. With a sickening sound of ripping flesh, Bestiality,

Pedophilia, and Slavery pulled an appendage from Terror. They cackled hysterically, waving around arms and legs,. What was left of Terror fell over, and they jumped on him until he was stomped into oblivion. The three demons were angry that their fun was over, but Slavery reminded them that Terror's torture would continue forever in the abyss.

A QUICK TRIP to the grocery store after work, I thought. I grumbled to myself as the customer in front of me in the check-out line was having some problem. *Uh-oh,* I thought as the beleaguered clerk flipped on the switch above the register. The light above the cash register blinked on and off.

I looked down, and Nick was dutifully holding onto his side of the cart. *Now what was Jon up to?* I thought with some irritation as he was no longer holding on to his side.

I looked behind me and started to say, "Jon, how many times do I have to tell you to hang onto the cart…"

Then I saw his face.

He was a picture of horror, about to run away. I was so tired, I must confess that I thought, *Oh no, now what?*

I softened my voice and said, "Honey, what's wrong?" He pointed mutely at a picture on a celebrity magazine at the top of the rack in the check stand. At first, I couldn't see anything out of the ordinary. Then I saw what he was staring at: A small inset picture of an apoplectic, furious man screaming with his mouth wide open. His entire face was red. I turned the magazine around in the rack so the guys could no longer see the picture, But I was suddenly on high alert.

Jon seemed to recognize this person.

Ever anxious to find more information to help find and prosecute the people who had abused my sons, I knelt and asked him in a whisper, "Who is that on the magazine?"

Jon looked all around with concern and then replied quietly, "Paul Blazer."

What?

Now I was the one holding up the line. I straightened up, apologized to those in line behind me and paid for my groceries. *I will have to come back another time when the boys aren't with me to purchase the magazine and give it to Perry.*

A few days later, I went to the grocery and picked up the magazine. The photo Jon had indicated was a little scary. The following day, the boys and I drove out to Detective Johnson's office. I sent the boys to the playroom so the Detective and I could have an adult conversation. Perry was responsive to my concerns, as always.

"Paul Blazer" was the name Jon gave me. "At least, that's what it sounded like to me," I said, mystified.

"Do you know anyone by that name?" Detective Johnson asked.

"No, I've never heard that name before, though I've been hearing about Matt and Sara since the beginning."

"I wonder if it could be a title rather than a name?" Detective Johnson said, thinking aloud.

Does he know more than he is telling me? I mused. *Another mystery. Will we ever have real answers?*

I pushed the cold bar on the door to exit the police station and shivered a bit as I ushered the boys back to the car.

And it was not just from the frigid air outside.

CHAPTER 21

"GUYS, I AM so excited we are going to the museum today. There are so many neat things to see," I said.

Jon asked, a little suspiciously, "Like what kind of things?"

"Cool stuff," I replied. "Like dinosaur bones, dioramas of how people used to live, displays of animals, rocks and minerals, and lots of stuff like that. I think you'll like it."

"Okay," he said unconvinced.

Oh good,' I thought as I parked, *it doesn't look too busy today.*

As we entered the museum, I held out our tickets to the docent. She smiled at Jon and Nick and said, "Welcome, Gentlemen! Is this your first visit to the museum?"

Jon said, "Yes. Is it fun?"

The docent replied, "My grandsons are four and six years old, and they love it. How old are you two?"

Jon and Nick looked to me, and I nodded that it was okay to respond. Nick held up four fingers and Jon said, "I'm five!" I smiled at the docent and then told Jon and Nick, "We need to stay together today, guys, okay?" They both nodded and we made our way into the museum.

"Wow! Look at that T-rex skeleton. It's huge!" I said.

"Is it real?" Jon asked. Nick was quite curious and went right up to the velvet rope surrounding the display. *So much for staying together,* I thought. But I was pleased to see his curiosity and enthusiasm.

"Yes, I believe it is. Let's see if we can read the sign over there," I suggested. Jon picked out some words he knew, and I read the rest. Nick was looking at the skeleton from every angle and finally said, "How does it stand up?"

"I'm not sure. Let's see if we can figure it out," I replied. We all looked around carefully and soon found wires coming down from the ceiling of the 2-story display area. Nick spotted some carefully hidden metal rods coming up from the floor through the legs. Their discovery was magical to them. I was so happy to see it.

"It's pretty amazing how they got all those bones together. Look at those teeth!" I observed. The exhibit didn't have a triceratops, Jon's favorite, but it did have a small stegosaurus, and Nick was delighted. "I can't believe they have my favorite dinosaur here!" Nick said.

I was thinking to myself, *Nick is speaking so much more since he and Jon have been working with Dr. Perez and not having the supervised visits. Jon's stuttering is so much reduced, I almost never hear it anymore. I am so thankful, Lord!*

"Look at all the gems and minerals in this hall, Guys!" I said with genuine enthusiasm. This was one of my favorite exhibits. To my dismay, Jon and Nick were not impressed with all the 'rocks.'

Strolling along with Nick close by, I saw Jon go a little ahead of us toward the Egyptology area. I was looking forward to seeing the exhibits there. I was about to call Jon back and remind him to stay with us as he went around a corner, out of sight.

Suddenly, I heard a small cry and Jon came flying back towards us with terror on his face.

My heart got cold and I stiffened in alarm. *Was his dad or one of the other abusers behind that wall? My body prepared to fight to protect my sons.* He was in such a blind panic, I thought he might run right through us.

"Jon, wait for us!" I cried. I wasn't sure he saw or heard me. As he started to go by in a panicked flight, I reached out and grabbed the hood of his jacket which he was wearing loosely. I knelt, pulled him into a hug and held on tight as he struggled to run on. It was at least a minute before he realized he was safe in my arms. Nick was mystified and went around the same corner before I could stop him. He came back with a shocked, horrified look on his face, but he was not in full panic mode as Jon had been.

"Okay, Guys. It's going to be alright," I said, trying to soothe them with my voice. "Let's go sit on the bench way over there at the other end of the hall." Sitting down on the cold, stone bench, I put one son on each knee and we had a good, long group hug. When they had calmed a bit, I said, "What did you see that was so scary?"

"Th...th-there's an Indian b-b-box, M...M-Mommy. Why would they have an Indian b-b-box h-here?" Jon asked, stuttering worse than I could remember him doing in weeks, maybe months.

I thought to myself, *it still amazes me how things can go from normal and routine to terrifying and crazy in a matter of seconds.* "Let's pray for Jesus' protection, okay?" I asked them aloud. Both boys nodded with solemnity. I held them tight and asked Jesus, "Please protect us and keep us safe. Thank You, Lord!" I felt both boys' bodies relax a bit.

I have to know what is around that corner, but I am not taking them with me to look. I looked at the corner in question and back to where we were sitting; a short distance. There was no one else in the hall right now. "Guys, I'm going to take a look. I need to see what was so scary for you," I said quietly. I kept my voice calm as I gave them the news.

"N...N...No, M-M-Mommy! D-D-Don't go b...b...back there!" Jon stuttered, his voice full of tears. Nick nodded in agreement, his eyes very wide.

"I'm not going back there," I reassured them. I'm just going to look around the corner. You'll be able to see me, and I'll be able to see you the whole time. You two sit right here together. This will just take a couple of seconds."

Moving quickly down the short hall, I turned and waved, and they waved back with obvious reluctance. I poked my head around the corner and saw a beautifully painted sarcophagus. It was closed, standing on end and leaning against a wall, heralding the entrance to the Egyptology exhibit. It looked like other Egyptian artifacts I had seen. But as I was finding, some relatively common-place objects took on new meanings in the world the boys had been forced to inhabit. I turned to face the guys and waved to show them I was still safe. They gestured with urgency for me to come back, while looking around with anxiety evident on their faces. As I crossed the short distance back to them, I puzzled in my mind, *Indian box? Why and where would they have seen something like this and why was it so frightening?*

"D...D...Did you see it?" Jon whispered; his eyes very wide.

"Yes, I did. Let's go back to the dinosaurs and see about getting some lunch. Would you like that?" I asked.

"Yeah!" they both answered.

As we walked back to the front of the museum, I wondered, *how do I approach THIS one?*

Revelations from Nick and Jon, I had discovered, could be a minefield. Treading carefully, attempting to understand without frightening them again or worse, having them 'shut down,' I had to keep things light. I asked a few general questions about the dinosaurs and other parts of the museum. I eventually worked my way around to the subject of the 'Indian box' as we munched on hamburgers and potato chips. I couldn't really taste mine because I felt upset, angry, mystified, and as usual, wondering how much worse things would get.

"So, Guys, what can you tell me about the "Indian box?" I asked in a quiet voice. They both looked at me with puzzled looks on their faces. It was one of several times that I got the impression they thought I was 'in on' what they had experienced. I felt a flash of anger at those people who had systemically removed every source of trust, comfort and any shred of safety from their minds. The abusers and Greg had been successful convincing the boys that there was no one they could trust. From the imposters in police and doctor uniforms—right up to their own mother.

"Y...Y...You don't know?" Jon asked with not a little incredulity in his voice.

"No, I honestly don't, but I want to understand why it was so scary for you," I said. The boys exchanged looks with each other, and I saw Nick nod as if giving Jon permission to tell me. Jon looked all around us. There was no one nearby to hear him tell me his secret.

"Jon, why is it called an 'Indian box?'" I asked.

Shrugging his little shoulders in fear, he said, "That's what Matt and Sara call it."

I started to ask, "Why is it so scary for you?" but thought better of it and instead asked, "Where did you see it before you saw it here today?"

"At Matt and Sara's."

"Was it in their house?"

"Yeah," he said. This was hard for him, but he was trusting me.

"In the kitchen?" I teased him a bit with a smile.

"No, where we watch the movies," he said. He had an expression that conveyed sadness and a little uncertainty that I did not already know about all of this. Nick was as quiet as he could be. My blood felt chilled when I remembered their initial revelations and how difficult it had been for them to tell me. I could tell his interest in our conversation was waning, and I wanted to tread carefully.

As I considered how to phrase another non-threatening question, Jon suddenly said, "They put Nick in the 'Indian Box,' closed the lid, and sat on it while he was crying and kicking. They wouldn't let him out." Jon's next words came out in a rush, "I tried to pull them off the box to let Nick out and they got mad at me and put me in a trash can." Jon's eyes were troubled as he remembered. They weren't teary or angry, just sorrowful beyond what any child his age should have the experience to be able to express.

"A trash can?" I asked, too surprised to even feel the rage about to spike. It was all I could think to say.

"Yeah, I had to scrunch up my legs. And it smelled really bad," Jon said. "Then they put the lid on, and it was too dark," Jon's voice broke a little as he went further into the memory.

I couldn't help myself, I had to ask, "Honey, where was your dad?"

"I yelled and cried, and he opened the lid. They were all laughing. Then they put the lid back on. I…I had to stay in there all night," Jon said, starting to cry. Nick patted his arm. I pulled him tight to me and told him, "I am so sorry. No one will ever hurt you again." I realized, even as I said it, I couldn't guarantee it.

Then I thought, *No, I can't protect them from all harm and hurt, but God can.* I breathed a silent prayer for protection over Jon and Nick, for now and in the future.

THAT LOCAL GROUP was so easy to manipulate: so greedy for power, sex and money, Stalker thought with characteristic cynicism. He chortled as he remembered commanding them to get the coffin-shaped box and paint it with 'special' symbols and colors. *Ha-ha!* They really believed that the designs would make a difference in power and effectiveness for them. *Ridiculous humans!* His ability to 'motivate' this particular group of pathetic humans had moved him up in the hierarchy. *As if their silly attempts at the worship of my master would garner them anything.* He laughed aloud, thinking about that.

He did have to admit that they followed directions quite well that night. Putting the younger innocent in the sarcophagus was a true amusement for Stalker. He gave them a small bit of power then. But they didn't follow through with the sacrifice. They were supposed to kill him then, by burning the sarcophagus. They sacrificed a breeder baby instead, which was acceptable, but their power gain was minimal.

Putting the older kid in the trash can was stupid beyond words. It made a huge negative impact on the boy, and caused him to have believable information about the specifics of some of the abuse. *What if he shared that story with someone?* Stalker wondered.

Suddenly, dread gripped the demon. He shook in abject fear. *What is happening?* he wondered, incredulous.

Since he had moved up in the ranks, he felt this assignment was beneath him. Following that clueless woman and her offspring around while listening to their conversations was laughably easy. He had long since stopped doing the assignment himself since nothing ever happened. It was boring and somewhat painful to be around the woman and her friends, especially that counselor she was seeing.

One of his subordinates was gibbering madly at him. *Just what was the stupid underling trying to say?* he thought with annoyance. The junior demon spoke again.

He froze, shocked. "Are you sure?" Stalker said, raising himself to his full height and towering over the shaking underling. "What do you mean they told their mother about the sarcophagus? They don't even know that word." Stalker raised his fist threateningly. The terrified underling managed to squeak out what he had overheard. He dropped the demon, who crumpled beneath him.

Now it was Stalker's turn to shake in fear.

"Why didn't you stop that kid, distract him or something? Did she believe him?" He answered the question before the underling had a chance to speak. "Of course she did. She always believes them." Stalker had a sinking feeling on the inside. Now she had valuable information about a ceremony even though she didn't know it.

Yet.

Stalker began to mutter to himself and walk about in crazy circles. *Now what will I do? How can I work this to my advantage? It wasn't my fault. What will Murder say about this?* "What am I going to do?" he growled.

The underling attempted to sneak away and find a place to hide.

He almost succeeded when, all at once, Stalker came out of his fugue and spotted the underling's careful movement.

"Where do you think you are going? If you had done your job, we wouldn't be in this fix!" Stalker screamed. "You will stay here and explain your failure to Murder, or I will banish you!" he threatened.

Chapter 22

WHAT A NAME—*The Center for Adult Survivors of Satanic Child Abuse*, I thought. As we drove there, my mind processed a whirlwind of thoughts while the boys slept. *I don't know why I'm not more excited. I admit I am a little curious. There will be people there who believe us and understand what we are going through. I won't have to spend time trying to convince someone that satanic abuse actually exists before we can get down to work. I've heard so much, so many revelations...I wonder if there can possibly be any more.* Even as I ask myself the question, I know the answer. *God help me, I am so weary of this. But I won't give up until the boys are safe. Maybe it will bring the boys some peace to talk to someone who is a grownup survivor,* I thought with some hope.

Pulling into the parking lot, I said, "Wake up, guys. We're here." *I'll bet no one suspects the secrets contained in this nondescript office building.*

Opening the door for a couple of still sleepy boys, I saw a smiling man coming down the hall towards us. Usually the guys shrank back a bit when meeting an unfamiliar male, but they didn't seem frightened at all. I hoped this was the man we had come to meet.

"Hi, I'm Mike," he said.

"Hi, I'm Elizabeth. This is Nick, and this is Jon," I replied, pleased to see them extend their hands to shake without prompting from me. *They are really growing up,* I thought with, I confess, a bit of pride.

Leading the way to a small conference room, Mike ushered us inside. There was nothing in the room but a table with a few books on it, two chairs, and a whiteboard with markers. "Hey Guys, did your mom tell you why we are getting together to talk today?" Mike asked in an easy manner.

"She said you are *another* therapist," Jon said with a little exasperation in his voice. I had to chuckle as did Mike.

"We've seen lots of different therapists," I explained.

Nick spoke up. "Dr. Perez is the best one," he said in a grown-up, serious voice.

"I'm not surprised you think so," said Mike. "He's a good friend of mine and an excellent therapist." Both boys brightened up a bit when they heard that. "He's the one who suggested to your mom that you come to see me," Mike explained. I could see the boys relaxed at that knowledge.

"There's something you should know about me–" Mike started to say when Jon broke in and said with a suspicious note in his voice, "Is it a secret?"

"No, it's not a secret. Lots of people know this about me." Mike reassured them. "Secrets can be a problem sometimes, right?" he said.

Both boys nodded solemnly and looked at me. I smiled to reassure them and said, "No more secrets, right, Guys?" They both nodded again, then Jon said, "Except Christmas and birthday presents, right, Mommy?"

"Right," I said with a chuckle and a little wink.

Mike smiled and continued, "Some people hurt me when I was just about your age. I really hated it."

Jon and Nick looked at each other with surprise.

"What happened to you?" Jon asked.

Mike answered, "Some of the same things that happened to you, I think."

Jon and Nick cast sidelong glances at each other. I could sense that they were starting to shut down. If they were going to benefit from this, they needed to re-engage. *What would be the best way?* The still, small voice said, "Tell them the truth."

"Do you guys remember when Dr. Perez and I asked you two if it would be all right for him to talk to someone who might help us?" I asked them. "That someone is Mike," I said with a smile. Both boys seemed to take a moment to deliberate, but then they relaxed again. Mike shot me a grateful glance over their heads.

Mike tried a different approach and asked them, "What do you remember most about what happened to you?"

Nick and Jon looked at each other. They barely knew this man. Would they open up? I said a silent prayer. After another moment, Nick nodded almost imperceptibly. I would have missed it had I not become accustomed to watching for such subtleties.

"Well, the people all wore robes," Jon started, watching for Mike's reaction.

"What kind of robes, like bathrobes?" Mike asked.

Jon looked a bit surprised and said, "No they were white robes with hoods over their faces.

"Yes, I do remember that. Did you ever touch the robes?" Mike responded.

"No!" they almost yelled in unison. My stomach dropped when I heard their fear.

Nick shook his head vigorously. "They told us not to ever touch their robe!" he said.

"Don't touch," Jon added.

"Why were they in the robes?" asked Mike. "What did they do in them?"

"They just stood around doing some funny singing," Jon started. "And they passed around a bowl with blood soup and they all drank some and they made us drink it too. It tasted very bad, but we were spanked if we spit it out and then they made us drink it again. Then I felt sleepy…" Jon's words were coming out in a jumbled rush. He took a short pause, then started again, pushing himself to say everything. "They had a big, black scary table they put the babies on. And one time they put a grownup on the table and they cut his neck off." Jon said breathlessly.

My mind reeled, but Mike appeared to be unfazed. His demeanor was open. He obviously believed them. He wasn't shocked or scandalized by the horrors they mentioned. This openness encouraged Jon and Nick, and they both started talking at once.

"The people were lying on each other—"

"—and uncovering their bottoms–"

Suddenly, as if a button were pushed, the boys stopped short. They both stared at me with an unfathomable expression on their faces.

"What's wrong, Guys?" I asked, trying to keep my face free of the horror and nausea rising inside of me.

After a moment, Jon whispered, "They said you would die if we ever told anyone."

"We're sorry we told," added Nick. They began watching me with great concern.

My horror was replaced by barely containable rage. *Not only did these people abuse them,* I thought, *but they had forced these little boys to carry a huge, terrible secret for all those months–to protect me! No wonder their pediatrician questioned why they hadn't grown physically for a year. All their energy was being used to keep that horrible lie!*

I focused on the boys, sending them as much love as I could without moving or saying a word. I would carry this burden for them now.

"Oh Honey," I said. "I'm *fine*. And they were so wrong to do those things to hurt you and make you keep secrets." I pulled both boys into my lap and said, "Remember, we are protected by Jesus. There is no one stronger than Jesus and He loves us more than we can imagine."

"That's right," Mike said. I squeezed the boys to me and felt the weight of that secret fall off of them. The fear. The sadness.

The hurt. It wasn't all gone, but the secret no longer tortured them. After a long moment, Mike asked, "Do you guys want to talk some more?"

Jon looked at Mike and asked, "Is this what happened to you?"

Mike gave them a sad look and said, "Yes, pretty much the same. But the people who hurt me wore black robes and one of them had a big, ugly hat."

Jon asked, "Did his hat have horns and a big tongue on it?" Nick nodded as they both looked at Mike intently.

"Did it look like a cow?" Mike asked.

"No, it had a skinny face with hair on its chin," Jon replied.

I could see Mike was being very careful not to lead the boys while still helping them understand that he had experienced similar things and was better now. That gave me a little more hope than the moment before.

THE CAVERN WAS in an uproar.

Myriads of demons were nervously fidgeting, pushing and shoving. Rumors flew about like sooty moths. There was bad news and that often meant some demons would cease to exist. Fear surged through the ranks like an incoming tide.

"I heard that some kids are telling things that should be kept secret," one demon said to the demon next to him.

"Somebody didn't do their job putting enough fear in them," the other judged. "Is it that one family we've been hearing about? The father's family have kept the secret and provided generations of entertainment for us. What happened this time around?" he asked with a large dose of disdain.

Another demon close by said, "I hear it was our Enemy intervening on their behalf. That's just not fair," he whined. "Our exalted leader was given this world to rule by man himself. He should be able to do with it whatever he wants. Not fair, not fair, not fair!" pouted the whiny demon, his voice becoming more irritating with every syllable.

Four or five demons nearby turned on him in the ranks, torturing him gleefully.

"Maybe you should have stayed in Heaven when we left," one of them spat.

"BE GONE!" they screamed in unison.

Howling in terrified mental anguish and physical pain, the whiny demon winked out of existence. The remaining demons laughed, yet kept a suspicious eye on each other.

"WOULD YOU TELL me about the big table?" Mike asked.

"It was black and shiny," Jon said.

I felt an electric shock go through me. I remembered an incident from a couple of years ago. Things were going pretty well; our lives had been calm of late. The cousins were playing in the bed of Jim's small pickup truck which was parked in my driveway when Nick fell out. He was crying and complaining that his shoulder area was hurting. I was concerned that he might have broken his collarbone.

Jim and I took Nick to the ER while Brenda watched the rest of the kids. Everything was fine until they called us into the x-ray room. The table was very modern, shiny and black instead of the usual silver. Nick took one look at that table and nearly ran through me trying to get out of the x-ray room. I scooped him up and placed him on the table. He was terrified and seemed exceptionally strong, as he fought to get away, crying, and screaming in terror. I had a hard time holding him and told the x-ray tech to hurry and take the picture, just so he could see we weren't going to hurt him.

The tech complied, though the look on his face told me he had no idea what was going on with the little boy acting that way. The x-ray whirred quietly and then stopped, and was mostly of me half on top of Nick.

I picked Nick up and held him as I explained about the pictures.

"If you lie very still for just one more minute, he will take another picture and we'll be done, OK?" I asked him with as much reassurance as I could muster. Nick nodded tearfully and lay down on his back, closing his eyes in resignation. We got the x-ray and I carried him quickly out of the room. I wasn't particularly surprised when the doctor said his collarbone, shoulder, and upper arm were all fine. After wrestling with him to get the x-ray, I was convinced and grateful that nothing was broken.

I shook off the memory, but as Jon continued his description, my blood ran cold.

"The table was very cold and sometimes had blood on it. The robe-people would get very excited when someone put a baby up there. The baby cried and cried and then it was quiet.

Mike nodded sympathetically and asked, "Could you see the top of the table from where you were?"

"Only if somebody held us up. It was gross. They told us the same thing would happen to us if we told anybody," Jon responded.

Mike went over to the whiteboard and asked the Guys to join him. He had a box of dry erase markers and let the boys each choose one. They were excited because we hadn't had markers at our house since the 'let's color the wicker seats of the kitchen chairs' incident.

Dry erase markers do not "erase" out of wicker—oh well.

Mike asked if Jon and Nick could remember anything that was on the table before they put the baby on it. "Yeah, there were big candles," Jon said.

Mike drew some tall tapers on the whiteboard and said, "Like this?"

Nick spoke up this time and said, "They were fancy on the bottom."

I realized, as Mike already suspected, that they were describing ornate candlesticks with candles in the top. Mike invited Nick to "correct" his drawing.

"OK, anything else?"

Nick continued, "There was a big knife." Nick looked at me to see if I had a reaction to this latest information. I did my best to keep my face neutral but encouraging.

"Where should I put that?" Mike asked. Nick pointed to a spot between the candlesticks and Mike drew what looked like a small paring knife.

"No," said Jon vehemently. "It was this big and drew a line nearly the length of the whiteboard. Mike drew something like a large sword and both boys nodded in approval.

"Wow, you two have good memories. Anything else?"

Nick said, "Don't forget the book!"

Mike picked up a largish textbook from a nearby bookshelf and asked, "Was it this big?"

The boys indicated with their hands that it was wider, longer, and thicker.

I could tell the guys were getting tired. With their afternoon nap interrupted to make this appointment, and all the emotional disclosures, they were running out of steam.

I was too.

Luckily the drawing was soon completed. I thought it would be a good place to give the boys a break. I completed my sketch of the whiteboard details.

"Hey guys, I think it's time to get going. Can you get your jackets, please," I requested.

Mike nodded, looking at me with sadness and sympathy. "I'll send you a copy of the report I send to Tom Perez," he said. "I'll also include some articles you may find helpful."

"Thank you, I appreciate your help," I said, shaking a bit as I put my coat on. Mike spoke to me in a soft voice, out of earshot of the boys, "Has anyone suggested that you all go into hiding?"

Just as quietly, I responded, "Yes. The police did. We're currently in a safe place, unknown to their father and his family. I'm extremely careful that I am never followed home."

"Please get in touch with me if you need any help," Mike said in earnest.

"Thank you. I will," I said. Nick and Jon were walking out the door ahead of me, evidently feeling bigger, better, and braver.

"Hey Guys, wait for me," I said, and they turned to wait for me.

"Mommy, are we going to McDonald's?" Jon asked.

"Indeed, we are," I replied, thinking that some 'normal' would be good about now.

CHAPTER 23

"**M**RS. PHILLIPS?" A voice said on the phone.

"Yes," I said with some caution.

"This is Jill, your new social worker."

"Hello, Jill," I replied. I felt nausea and anxiety start to crawl up my legs into my stomach and back.

"Mrs. Phillips, I need to inform you that Social Services has dropped the case against your ex-husband," Jill said with what sounded like regret in her voice.

What? My mind exploded. *They did what? I can't believe that!* "WHY?" I said. "They can't do that! This is impossible! What are we supposed to do now?" I implored my latest social worker while sharp, hot tears stung my eyes, sliding down my face like molten lava. My knees felt like jelly. Considering the ramifications, I was buffeted by wave after wave of suffocating fear, dread, and anxiety.

"I'm going to do some investigating and I'll get back to you," Jill said. "You should call your attorney."

I ended the call, hung up the phone, and slumped to the floor. "How can this be, Lord? Aren't you going to protect them anymore? *Please!* Help us, Lord!" I cried out loud through my tears.

Once I stopped crying, I called Zach Taylor, my attorney at his office. I explained what I had just learned from the social worker and reminded him of the results of our most recent hearing.

Greg was offered a 'plea bargain' of sorts. He was to be evaluated and undergo treatment in return for a 'no-fault' finding for him in the case. The deal fell apart when he refused, yet again, to comply with the orders of the court. *I couldn't understand his attitude although I couldn't complain about the results,* I thought. *If he really wanted to see the boys as much as he claimed to, I would have thought he would do whatever necessary.*

Evidently, the case was totally mishandled by the bumbling county attorney. The consequences of noncompliance for Greg's third failed plan of court-ordered evaluation and treatment were clear. They were to set the case for trial and begin the case again. But for some reason, the judge allowed Social Services to drop the case. *Was there some kind of interference going on with our case in court?*

In dismissing the case, the judge apparently said it "needed a new start." He sent it to the domestic (divorce) court to work out visitation. *My attorney and I were not invited to this latest hearing. Was Greg there?* I wondered.

On hearing the news, I was devastated. Beyond hopeless. The information was so shocking, I began shivering.

Without the Social Services case, the judge in this heavily "joint custody" state would have no reason to deny unsupervised visitation. If that occurred, I was afraid we would never see the boys again, especially because I had caused Greg so much trouble in the past months.

As the evening passed, I prayed intermittent prayers. "God, why, after all we've been through, does the enemy appear to have won? How will I protect my sons?" A sleepless night full of tears followed.

Are we going to be forced to go underground?

Later, I heard a song that perfectly described my feelings:

"The Warrior is a Child"

By Twila Paris

Lately I've been winning battles left and right
But even winners can get wounded in the fight

People say that I'm amazing
I'm strong beyond my years
But they don't see inside of me
I'm hiding all the tears

[Chorus]
They don't know
That I come running home when I fall down
They don't know
Who picks me up when no one is around?
I drop my sword and cry for just a while
Cuz deep inside this armor
The warrior is a child

Unafraid because his armor is the best
But even soldiers need a quiet place to rest
People say that I'm amazing
I never face retreat
But they don't see the enemies
That lay me at his feet

[Chorus]
They don't know
That I come running home when I fall down
They don't know
Who picks me up when no one is around?
I drop my sword and look up for His smile
Cuz deep inside this armor (deep inside)
Deep inside this armor
Deep inside this armor
The warrior is a child

Oh, the wonderful power of music to soothe me!

I had no more tears, and I was now able to hear the still, small voice speaking to me again.

"What did I promise you?" God asked in response to my prayers.

I thought back and remembered the promise given near the beginning of the case. "You promised that everything was settled, and the boys and I were free!" I said with a sullen attitude.

"Has anything really changed?" He asked. The loving tone of His voice caused me to stop and reconsider my attitude. "Do you trust me?" He asked.

"Wow," I said. Then I considered it further and said in a loud voice, "I do trust You, Lord!" The statement cleared the cobwebs and I stated, "You alone are worthy of praise! You are my strong fortress and my high tower, and I choose to believe that You are going to keep Your promise to us!"

I felt better than I had since I'd heard the devastating news. *This is what faith is all about,* I told myself. *I have no idea what's going to happen, but I know that God loves us and cares for His children. The victory is His!*

THE MOOD IN the cavern was maniacally jubilant. Underlings were still destroyed at the usual rate, but among the hierarchy, there was much self-congratulation going on.

"We won!" They shouted all over the cave. "That stupid Christian for all her faith, has proven no match for our scheming. Take that, God! Our master is just as powerful as You without the annoying complications of Your love for those humans," Mid-level demons were all talking at once, all over each other. "Our master controls the courts and they are finally coming into line with our desires!"

Pride, the highest-ranking demon present, wasn't saying much.

He stood looking on at all the frenetic activity. But he had to admit, he felt uncharacteristically unsettled. He flinched a bit under the assault of that woman's voice in battle. Her growing faith was a real problem. The others weren't paying attention. Their overconfidence was going to doom their efforts to failure. However, Pride still had a few tricks to try and his praise from the master would be all the sweeter since he wouldn't have to share it with anyone.

Just for fun, he banished the nearest underling. He left the celebration so he could continue pondering his next steps.

CHAPTER 24

"Y<small>EAH</small>, M<small>OM</small>, J<small>ON</small> loves his new kindergarten class," I shared during one of what I referred to as "support" phone calls. After a while, she and Daddy didn't feel the need to call every night. But we still spoke several times a week or when there was a new development in the case.

"It seems like your circumstances have calmed down a bit," she said. I could almost hear the smile in her voice. "What is Nick up to today?"

"He is on a play date with Daniel. He gets lonely when Jon is at school, and I trust Darlene implicitly."

"What about Greg? Has he bothered you lately?" Her tone was neutral, but I knew she was still very upset about his behavior.

"No, not in a while," I said. "I'd like to hope we're done with all that, though I doubt it. But God continues to grow my faith in little ways each week. Well, I've got to get the kitchen straightened up before Nick comes home. Love you, Mom. Talk to you soon!"

"Bye, Elizabeth. We love you."

That morning, I was trying to pray but having trouble concentrating. Being without the guys, even for just a few hours at a time, was difficult. *I think I'll take a walk and pray,* I told myself, *since I can't seem to keep my focus on the Lord this morning.*

I put on shoes and headed out the door; the neighborhood was quiet. With the kids in school and most of the people at work, the cul-de-sac was deserted. I felt very safe walking in our neighborhood.

Greg knew nothing about this location. Unafraid, I walked to the corner and crossed the street.

Just as my right foot stepped up on the opposite curb, I heard the still, small voice speaking to me. *"You are to go to Montana,"* He said very clearly.

What? I thought. *This must be wishful thinking. I've been praying to escape from here for over two years now, and the answer has always been, "No."*

It was only then that I realized—maybe His repetitive "No" was actually "Wait and trust Me."

As I continued to walk along, I mused on this new understanding. *Could I really trust the still, small voice?* I had become confident in His direction over the last two years, but this was something I really wanted. As if on cue, the rush of questioning thoughts bombarded my reasoning. *What if I was just making this up in my head? And what about Dr. Perez; Jon and Nick's therapy, Jon's school, our church, my job? And how would I ever get away from Greg? Could I even do this legally?*

The protective orders were still in place. The divorce decree stated neither their father nor I could take them out of state permanently without the written consent of the other. Requesting Greg's permission would be an exercise in futility, and I didn't want to make waves. But the family court failed to continue protecting my sons. By not following through on the consequences of my ex-husband's continued flaunting of the court orders, the jurisdiction for the case ultimately fell into the divorce court.

There was little hope, except for one thing: My God was still Sovereign, and I believed He would continue to protect the boys. I turned around at my usual halfway point and headed back to my house. It would soon be time to pick Nick up from Daniel's house. When we got back, he and I would go to meet Jon's school bus. The afternoon was busy, so I was distracted for the rest of the day. Later that night, after the boys went to bed, I started thinking some more about the astonishing news I felt Holy Spirit had given me that morning.

I had to admit, I was so excited!

In my usual "Martha-esque" style, I started planning and organizing, at least in my thoughts. I was getting mentally 'wound up' in my 'what ifs' when the Mary (Martha's sister who chose to listen to Jesus instead of anything else) part of my brain made a suggestion.

You don't have a clue yet how to obey this or what to do first, so how about doing some listening before deciding or doing anything?

Partly excited and partly fearful, it was another night of very little sleep. I confess I was rattled and sleepy the next day at work.

Our department usually went to break together after we drew the morning laboratory blood samples for the hospital patients. I got my tea and bagel with cream cheese and jelly as I usually did. I had hoped it would help me wake up. As I approached the table where my friends were seated in the hospital cafeteria, out of my mouth fell this question, "Is it Ash Wednesday?"

My friends were taken aback since it was mid-January–and a Friday. I tried to chuckle it off, but it was bizarre. Since I didn't grow up in the Catholic church, I had never celebrated Ash Wednesday in my life. I knew about the practice but had never thought much about it.

"Wow, I hope that tea helps," said the only other tea-drinker at the table.

Juanita was Catholic and chuckled as she kindly corrected, "Today is Friday, and Ash Wednesday isn't until next month." I was embarrassed but she just patted my arm and said, "Don't worry, we all have those days."

As soon as I picked up the boys and arrived at home, I went immediately to the calendar I had hung on the inside of the pantry door. I turned the page to February, and on the box for the date of February 28, "Ash Wednesday" appeared.

OK, what was the significance of this? I wondered. *Could this be the date we are to leave to go to my parents' home in Montana?*

I still wasn't convinced.

I called my Bible study friends and asked for prayer for an 'unnamed request.' I didn't dare talk to anyone about my so-called plan for fear that the courts or Greg would put an end to it. Only in my prayer and personal time, I nurtured this wonderful idea I had grown to like.

Over the next several days, I had gained confidence that this 'leading' was truly from the Lord. I called my brother, Jim, and told him what I had been thinking. His initial response was pretty close to my first thoughts: *Can I get away with this? Is this a good idea?* But as we talked a while, he began to get excited about it, too.

"Here is what I suggest," he said. "Why don't you collect a few boxes and put things in them that you would feel O.K. about leaving here, in a storage unit. Have you spoken with your attorney yet?"

"No," I admitted. "I was afraid he would tell me, 'No way.'"

"Well, you won't know until you ask, right?" he said. "He must keep it confidential. You know him well enough to be confident that he will, right?"

"Yes," I said, nodding as I spoke over the phone. As if Jim could see it. "I don't worry about that. I initially thought about not telling anyone so that if it became a legal issue, you and everyone else could honestly deny any knowledge of what I was planning. But I slipped in my counseling appointment with Grace and told her about it. She said she would pray, and that I should talk to you about it." I confided.

"Good advice," my brother said quietly. "I want to help as much as I can. Here's another thought; as you are starting to do some preliminary packing, think about priorities. Boxes for storage, label those #3; things it would be nice to take along but not essential, #2 and basic necessities, label those #1. And let me know what your attorney thinks, Okay?"

When I called him, the query to my attorney, Zach Taylor, brought an enthusiastic assent. "I think that's a great idea," he said brightly. "Let me do some research and get back to you so we can know for sure."

A few days later, he called and said, "It looks like we're in a grey area here. Social Services dropped the case, inappropriately, I might add. So, you are no longer under their jurisdiction except that the protective orders are still active under family court. The domestic courts have your divorce decree with the prohibition against leaving the state, but they have not entered into the case yet."

Is this God's provision? I wondered.

He continued. "We haven't received any requests for hearings or visitation from your ex-husband. So, for right now, I can't see any reason why you can't leave. But the domestic court could cite you for contempt if your ex-husband pushes it," he finished.

I ended the call and immediately called Jim, relating the information to my brother.

"Aren't you worried about being held in contempt of court?" Jim asked.

"No," I said, sure of myself. "I think any place away from here would be better. Besides, I believe God told me to move, so I know He will provide for us," I replied. "I'll worry about the courts later."

So, I began the preparations for the move.

CHAPTER 25

LYING IN BED, I took a few moments to try to catalog my thoughts.

I wish I could say that everything was smooth sailing after I made the decision to go ahead and make the move to Montana with the boys. I still vacillated day-to-day and sometimes, hour-to-hour, operating in secrecy and sometimes in fear. Until I remembered one event from two years prior. That memory of Nick's unshakeable faith in my ability to get us safely across the busy street got my attention and built my faith again.

I have often returned to that picture in my mind of his little hand reaching up, knowing I would be there. And it is as true and vivid today as it was on that sparkling autumn morning over two years ago.

It says in God's Word (Isaiah 41: 10 and 13 NIV):

So, do not fear, for I am with you;

do not be dismayed, for I am your God.

I will strengthen you and help you;

I will uphold you with My righteous right hand.

For I am the Lord your God

Who takes hold of your right hand

And says to you, 'Do not fear; I will help you.

All I must remember to do is to put my hand up, so He can hold it.

That same autumn, after we had moved, Grace, my counselor, told me God had indeed kept us safe. She discerned in the Spirit as she was doing battle for us that there was another plan to get the boys and sacrifice one or both on Halloween, satanism's highest "holy" day.

She continued to battle for us and didn't tell me until after the first week in November, so I wouldn't be paralyzed in terror.

PRIDE CONSIDERED CONSULTING with Murder about his idea. But he knew that Murder would steal all the credit when the master's plan for these two little boys was completed.

Pride was going to have to search to find those kids on his own. The other demons couldn't find them, but he was sure he could. Once he found them, he would have their dad kidnap them and sacrifice them on Halloween before anyone else was the wiser.

The master would be so appreciative that this blot on the record of the demonic horde was eliminated, he would undoubtedly reward Pride for his loyalty and brilliance. He would rise to the top of the hierarchy with lots of power. He would receive all the underlings he wanted to banish whenever he wanted, and a more human appearance, like the others high in the demonic hierarchy. No more scaly, misshapen arms and legs—he would appear like a human adult. Then, he could better undermine the efforts against his master of those wretched Christians.

After all, when the master won the final battle, Pride would be right in line to rule and reign. It was a natural choice for Pride to be one of those given a mighty crown on that glorious day.

I WAS so glad Grace had not told me about her discernment of this plan until after Halloween. When she shared her information with me, my body became numb and my mouth went totally dry.

After all of the things we had seen and experienced with the boys, this was the scariest yet. But out of it came the sense of blessing and joy that God had once again frustrated the plans of the enemy and would continue to do so.

I was thankful beyond words.

CHAPTER 26

MY FRIENDS AT work only occasionally teased me about my Ash Wednesday confusion. "Hey, Elizabeth, what day is it today?" they would inquire with a laughing tone over the next days and weeks.

But I was beginning to think that my question about Ash Wednesday was God giving me direction with my own voice. I had wondered how I would know what date to go. Still, I thought it would be good for Jon to complete his first year of school before leaving. I prayed a lot about this and finally decided that if ever there was a good time to uproot Jon during the school year, kindergarten would be it. Nick wouldn't be starting school until next fall. *Besides, I really didn't want to wait until June.*

So many details still needed to be addressed. I still hadn't told my parents we were moving (to their house, no less). My boss of fifteen years needed to know. And I needed to pretend nothing was going on, so the boys would not tell anyone.

"Escape Day" was still a month away, but God had to continually remind me that He had everything under control.

"Of course, we are thrilled, but..." Mom's voice trailed off.

"Is it legal for you to just leave?" My dad asked in a solemn voice from his phone.

"Zach told me it was a grey area, and I might face contempt of court charges. I still would rather be handling that stuff from an unknown location."

As if a switch were flipped, they both chimed in, "We can't wait to see you! Do you need any help?"

"Jim is helping me a lot. And Dr. Perez is moving out of state because of threats to him and his family. I don't want you two unnecessarily exposed to Greg's schemes.

I told close friends what I was planning so they could pray for me–I needed it. But I didn't tell Social Services, and I decided to wait to tell Detective Johnson until we were close to our leaving date. I wondered about informing the court, but since they had dropped the case, I decided that there was no one there who would care to know.

I was exhausted.

I felt like I was slogging through quicksand every day. Still working, keeping my "news" to myself, and packing boxes. It was hard organizing our belongings into 'ones', 'twos', and 'threes' so they could be packed appropriately while keeping it secret. I felt like I was running out of steam. It was so hard to keep things under wraps, and I nearly cried every time I thought about my little boys forced to keep horrible secrets so I wouldn't die.

I finally told the guys about our impending move at one of our after-counseling suppers.

"But what about Dr. Perez?" Jon asked.

"I already told Dr. Perez we would not be coming to counseling until we got settled in a new home. And you know what? Dr. Perez is moving too," I informed them.

"Is he okay?" Nick seemed worried as he asked the question.

"He is fine. He said he would miss you two, but you are both strong and brave now."

Jon replied with enthusiasm, "Everybody is moving. This is GREAT!"

Dr. Perez had surprised me when he told me he would be moving. In a conversation the boys were not privy to, he informed me that he was planning to leave. Dr. Perez was closing his practice and moving his loved ones to another state where his extended family lived because he was worried about his wife and children. He had received threats about continuing to treat the boys, and his office was being watched all the time by nefarious characters.

The timing would work out well for his move because it was, coincidentally, at the same time as when we were going. I was still sad about what he told me regarding his safety being jeopardy. He had evidently endured this in silence as long as he could. His receptionist, Wendy, would be out of a job. And all the children that needed his expert help would have to find assistance elsewhere.

I was sad for him but furious that Greg's selfishness and activities had caused so much disruption in so many peoples' lives. The next time he called to threaten Dr. Perez, he would get a disconnected number.

I had to confess that thought made me smile.

Over the two-and-a-half years following our initial visit to Dr. Perez, the little office became a place of comfort and healing. Of course, the exceptions were the visits the boys had with their father. Walking into the office on those days, the atmosphere was thick and black. It felt like driving a motorcycle into a brick wall without a helmet.

The boys and I prayed daily for Dr. Perez's family and protection for them. Dr. Perez taught me to trust people outside my immediate family to help me care for Jon and Nick. With many answered prayers and the diligent care of Dr. Perez, there was much healing for my young sons.

More and more, I was learning to trust God for provision too.

For example, Dr. Perez, after being convinced by the boys of my innocence in their trauma, worked with Detective Johnson. Because of their recommendations, the Crime Victims Fund paid for most of the fees for the boys' counseling. This required extra work for Dr. Perez in the form of reports to be submitted. But he seemed only too happy to do it.

Seeing Wendy became a weekly encouragement. She was so

kind and even sent me a Mother's Day card. It came at just the right time, with a note saying I was an excellent mom to my boys. I so needed it.

God's provision, again. And a stone of remembrance.

I also completed a small needlepoint picture of flowers in a repeating pattern over this period of time. It was a detail of a seventeenth-century tapestry. It is displayed, to this day, in my mom's home as another reminder of God's presence and victory.

Murder laughed uproariously. He was laughing so hard that his words came out in sputters.

"He t-thought what? After all the d-demons involved and all the f-failed plans, he was sure he could do it all alone? Pride is such an idiot!" He laughed again. "Besides, anything to do with sacrifice, of necessity, involves me," Murder asserted to no one in particular.

His sidekick, Suicide, remarked, "Don't forget our Enemy's strategies. He's always helping those stupid humans as soon as they ask." He changed the subject. "But there *is* one particular human who has been interfering long enough. The mom's counselor needs to be dealt with. She is actually the main one who foiled Pride's ridiculous plan. Send an underling to create fear and get rid of her."

It was Murder's turn to look askance at Suicide. "You don't think we've tried?" he said. "She and her husband are serious prayer warriors. And the people she has taught, including the mother, are now fighting to protect her," Murder yelled.

It was suddenly, eerily quiet in the cavern.

Within a moment, underlings were running toward the exit like lemmings. Murder reached out and grabbed one by the throat.

"Where are you going?" he rasped.

The underling was terrified, not an unusual state for them. "They're coming," he babbled.

"Who is coming?" Murder screamed, shaking the underling.

"Th...the...the le...le...leaders," the underling was finally able to stutter.

Murder looked around for Suicide, who was nowhere to be found.

"Suicide left me behind and didn't warn me," he muttered. "He'll pay for that. I'd better make myself scarce. Besides it was Pride who failed, not me," he said to no one in particular.

CHAPTER 27

O H *No!!* I thought. The soft-voiced woman on the phone said she was calling from Social Services. I didn't recognize her voice, and I didn't know why she was calling. There were stacks of boxes everywhere and I glanced around our townhouse filled with worry.

Wait, what did she say?

"I'd be happy to bring the boys down to your office," I stammered. "I'm sure that would be more convenient for you," I said, forcing myself to smile into the phone. Her response left me cold inside. "You need a home visit?" I replied to her repeated request.

"Umm, sure, if that's what you need, that will be fine. When would you like to come?" I spoke pleasantly, but I was feeling very panicked. "Tomorrow?" My worst fears bloomed in my stomach. *It's obvious we're moving, and there is too much already packed to do anything about hiding the fact from the Social Worker.*

She was talking again.

"Jon will be home from kindergarten at about one p.m.," I said, hoping I hadn't missed a part of her conversation.

I don't remember ending the call.

I thought back to when I had decided to move. I had confirmation from several prayer partners. God had given me peace and even told me the date I should leave. Now, I had a pinched nerve in my back and sciatic nerve that began screaming pain down my leg. *How was I going to pack up the entire townhouse and do the cleaning I needed to do? How did we accumulate so much stuff?* I worried. *Now, we might not be going anywhere!*

The still, small voice began speaking to me. "You and the boys will be free, just trust Me. Remember the story from the Holocaust? How Corrie Ten Boom told of the time her sister hid their Bible under her shirt?"

My mind snapped to the story. Corrie and her sister stood in a line for inspection. They were being moved from one concentration camp to another. Starving and very skinny; it was undeniable that her sister kept something sizeable under her shirt. Corrie prayed, and even though the guards looked right at her sister, they didn't seem to see the large lump. The sisters were cleared, and passed along to the next checkpoint."

God is in charge. The still, small voice of the Holy Spirit was a great reminder.

"Well then, Lord, I need you to hide these boxes in plain sight," I earnestly prayed before going to sleep. That night, I slept very soundly. I was at peace. In His perfect peace. Morning brought renewed concern and I prayed almost constantly, either silently or out loud. I only spoke out loud when Jon was at school and Nick was riding his bouncy horse in the playroom. *I hadn't broken it to Nick yet that his beloved bouncy horse would not be going with us. I dreaded talking to him about it.*

Two o'clock came, and the doorbell rang. Of course, the social worker was right on time.

I called the guys from the playroom and introduced them to the social worker. She was nice and quite soft-spoken, and Jon and Nick did an excellent job shaking her hand and saying "Hello" very politely. They asked to return to their play. I said it was fine, because the social worker said she wanted to talk just to me first.

I tried to relax so she wouldn't suspect a problem, but she didn't seem to notice my nervousness. She asked questions about how Jon was doing at school, how both the boys were doing in therapy, and general questions about our lives. I really hoped she wouldn't ask them if they were still in therapy since we had said "good-bye" to Dr. Perez the previous week. For the first time in two and a half years, they weren't in therapy.

She looked around at the living room and said, "Lovely home, are you moving?"

I answered honestly. "Yes, we are." Inside I cringed, waiting to see what she would do.

I was shocked.

"I hope you are moving a long way away," she said. "I can't tell you this officially, but out of state would be a good idea. I've read your case file, and you didn't hear it from me, but the family court cannot protect your sons from unsupervised visitation because the case has been sent to domestic court."

I started to tear up, and she patted my knee. "Will you be moving soon?" she asked

I nodded, not trusting to speak and keep the tears inside my eyes.

She said, "Great. The sooner, the better," and looked me square in the eye. "I'll say goodbye to the boys on my way out. Best of luck to you, dear."

I was so surprised by our conversation, I almost neglected to get up and see her to the door. I showed her the playroom, only partially packed, and she said goodbye to the boys.

Then she left.

I was so shocked, I stood there for a moment staring at the now-closed front door.

The next morning, I left a message for my attorney, Zach Taylor, and when he returned my call, he said, "That's good enough for me. I am really surprised by the Social Worker's reaction to the news that you are planning to move. I'll try to stall any demands from Greg's attorney for a day or so, if there are any. I would still be as sneaky getting out of town as you can."

The following day was Ash Wednesday.

Jim arrived about noon with a large truck complete with a trailer hitch for my car. I would be driving his pickup which he would use to drive back home. First, we loaded up my car, then Jim and I loaded the truck. We had decided to take everything along–all the ones, twos and threes. However, I had rented a storage unit near home in case we needed it. It would remain empty but rented in my name for two months.

Holy Spirit also said to leave my bank account open. I didn't know why then, but leaving it there would figure prominently in the future.

As the day progressed and the time to leave drew closer, I felt more scared than excited to finally be escaping this nightmare. But I was fearful that somehow, my ex-husband was going to find us and stop us–maybe hurt my brother or get the boys. There had been no activity on our block, and I had no discernible reason to fear. Greg didn't know where we were as far as I knew.

Pray, the still, small voice came into my head.

Oh yeah, that's what I should do when I'm afraid. You'd think I would have learned that by now.

We finished packing up the townhouse where we had moved when we left Chuck and Susan's home. I left the key in the kitchen and locked the door.

Never to return, I hoped.

Our little caravan was on the move. Jim drove the big truck with Nick riding shotgun. Jon rode with me. It would be a long drive to get to where we expected to spend the night. But the further we went from our old home, the better and freer I felt. For some reason, I kept thinking the police were going to pull us over and drag us back to town.

Pray and don't be afraid, the still, small voice clearly said in my head.

On we went, passing several police cars without incident.

We arrived at the planned motel very late, and everyone was tired. We had a quick supper and went right to bed. The next morning, Jon and Nick were wide awake very early. The boys were very excited but more relaxed than I had seen them in ages. I had a hard time convincing them to stay quiet in the motel room, since it was very early, because Jim promised waffles for breakfast. Once Jim got up, we met for breakfast. We looked at our options and decided, even though it was still two long driving days, we would drive straight through.

Eighteen hours later, at two a.m., we arrived at my parents' home and I felt physically safe for the first time in two and a half years.

God had indeed kept His promise.

I was so thankful.

Once Jim, the boys and I got to my parents' house, we all slept for four hours. Then Jim and I took all the stuff to the storage unit my dad had rented. I could not have done it without Jim's help. He got us settled and then took off in his pickup to drive back home that same day.

I was amazed at his stamina and prayed for God to protect him on the way back.

But more than that, I was overcome with indescribable *relief!*

CHAPTER 28

W E STAYED WITH my parents for several months.
I found a job, registered Jon for kindergarten, and found
a great before and after school sitter for Nick and Jon. We
moved to a condo near my parents' home and made new friends. We
even found a church we enjoyed and settled in. I remember thinking
this is crazy on one particularly hectic day. With baseball games after
work, snacks for the one team, needing a gift for a birthday party
the upcoming weekend, and very little time for supper.

The still, small voice said to me, *I answered your prayer for a regular,
normal life.*

Indeed, He had!

When I realized that, I had to chuckle. My heart was indeed full
of gratitude.

Everything was going well until I received a phone call early one
evening.

The caller identified himself as an agent of the Federal Bureau
of Investigation. He wanted to come to visit us at our home. Old
habits die hard, and I immediately went into panic mode. I started
praying, but I still felt so fearful. *Who was this person?* I thought. *Was
he really with the FBI? Did he want to drag us back to our old home? Was
this someone hired to kidnap the boys? Was he going to bring a court order
to take the boys back to our old home?* I couldn't stop the questions, it
seemed.

My family and I decided it would be wise to arrange to meet at my home, while the boys stayed with Grandma and Grandpa for a few hours, or longer if necessary.

The fateful day for the appointment arrived. I hadn't slept well for several nights thinking about it, so I was exhausted. I watched the clock irrevocably approach the time we had agreed upon. And just on the minute, the doorbell rang.

My stomach jumped in my throat as I went to answer the door. I breathed a silent prayer for help and opened the door.

There were two people at the door, a man and a woman. Both were dressed in dark business suits and offered me their identification before I could ask. I invited them in as cordially as I could, but I thought I might have to excuse myself to go throw up. As we made our way to the living room, I offered water and they both demurred. We sat down, and I had to remind myself to breathe. I realized I had been holding my breath most of the time since the doorbell rang.

"How can I help you?" I asked, trying to look them in the eye to assure them of my innocence.

"Are you the Elizabeth Anne Phillips who was married to Greg Phillips?"

"Yes, I am, but we are divorced now and have been for over 2 years."

"Mrs. Phillips, do you remember signing a federal form promising never to disclose anything your husband might have said in his sleep?"

"Yes, I do remember signing that form." *Ha! I couldn't help but remember.*

It was called the "pillow talk" contract. I recalled thinking it was kind of funny because I would never betray my country. That agreement was required of everyone who married someone with high-security clearance. Due to his federal job, Greg's clearance was among the highest.

By now, I was more mystified than frightened and asked, "What is this all about?" The two agents looked at each other, and the female agent said, "There is some concern about your husband's—'

"Ex-husband," I interrupted.

"Ah, yes. Sorry," the woman said, starting again. "Your ex-husband's security clearance is under review. There are some questions we hope you might be able to help us with."

"Is it true that your ex-husband was accused of child abuse and ritualistic satanic activity with the children?" The male agent said.

I went on high alert at the mention of the ritualistic satanic abuse. *That was only mentioned the one time*, I thought. *And Greg was the one who brought it up in court.* But those records should have been sealed.

My ex-husband worked at a government facility, or at least he used to. The FBI had been informed that child pornography and satanic material had been going through the interoffice mail at the facility. They didn't specify who was involved, but I got the impression that several people were being investigated.

The agents picked up on my discomfiture and backtracked a bit.

"Would you please tell us what happened in the court case, Mrs. Phillips?" the man asked.

I told the story from my perspective while wondering to myself, *what was going to happen now?*

After I finished giving them a brief, though honest explanation, there was an awkward silence. "What will happen to him?" I finally asked.

They explained that, once they concluded their investigation, he would probably have a hearing to see if he would retain his top-secret security clearance. Without that top-secret clearance, he would not be able to work at the facility—he would effectively be out of a job.

"Thank you for your time, Mrs. Phillips," the woman said as she stood. "I'm sorry for the trouble that this illegal, abusive activity has caused for you and your sons. Would you be willing to fly back for the hearing?"

"Absolutely," I said. My knees were shaking so hard with relief, I wasn't positive I could stand up Still, I managed to see them to the door.

As always, God protected us, and the FBI visit was just more evidence of that. They weren't coming to take Jon and Nick back after all.

I was so grateful, I couldn't stop smiling after they left. I called my parents right away.

"Hi, Mom! Daddy, are you on the phone too?"

"Elizabeth, what happened?" Daddy said. His tone of worry was evident, despite his typical stoicism.

"There's a chance Greg may lose his security clearance," I said with relieved excitement. The FBI has found evidence that child pornography and pictures of satanic stuff have been going through the inter-office mail at his plant."

"Oh, that's what they wanted. That's a relief! I was afraid you and the boys were going to have to run," Mom said with a humorless laugh.

The male agent said there would be a hearing unless my ex-husband decided not to contest the loss of his security clearance. Evidently, Greg did not want to have a hearing. I wondered, *why not? Was he concerned about what might be revealed?*

Some months later, I received notification that a hearing would not be held.

God's word to me was more real to me every day I spent in Montana. As He had said, "Everything was settled; the boys and I would be free."

Nothing was 'settled' to me. But I felt that we could get on with our lives.

Wow, was I ever wrong!

CHAPTER 29

THINGS WERE CALM for several months.

Then Greg went back to court in our old home state, and the court required me to supply our address and phone number. The next phase of our lives began with some letters designed to intimidate me.

Every time I saw his scrawled handwriting on an envelope in the mail, nausea rose up in my throat. The fear was still present, even multiple states away. I didn't want to open any of his missives, but I had to.

There were the usual threats–horrifying to read. He was going to get the boys. I could not get away with leaving the state with them. I was a terrible mother because I denied the guys the right to talk to and know their dad. And the scariest, something 'bad' was going to happen to me.

I was still under such fear of him that, even though I had learned to battle the enemy more effectively, I could feel my defenses start to crumble. I would only reply if necessary, and always politely. After that, I'd place his newest letter and envelope in my ever-growing file of contemporaneous notes, court notices, letters from various professionals, and my own journals.

I even received a threatening note from my ex-father-in-law.

He stated I was a terrible mother to keep my children away from their grandfather, and he didn't feel I was capable of raising the boys by myself. Then came the real topper: a letter from Greg demanding that I put four-year-old, Nick and five-year-old, Jon on a plane by themselves. He wanted my small children to go back to our previous home to celebrate their father's birthday. Never mind that he had totally ignored Nick's recent birthday.

This demand was laughable.

I replied the same day I received it. I politely told him there was no way I was going to put my two little boys on an airplane by themselves. I reminded him that he was still under orders of the court not to see the boys unsupervised. I also enclosed a copy of a newspaper article my dad had clipped out. It detailed the story of an eight-year-old unaccompanied child who was sexually molested on a recent flight.

I didn't think that would be the end of it.

Sure enough, another scary envelope arrived several days later. This envelope was from the county court. My hands shook as I opened it. I expected that the papers inside would say there was another hearing scheduled. I was shocked to find that the county court was holding me in contempt of court for leaving the state, and a trial date was scheduled in a few months!

Full-on panic ensued, despite all my experiences thus far (and my growing faith). All I could think was the courts were dragging me and my boys back, and their father would get his hands on them again. I continued 'awfulizing', thinking they would be sacrificed, and I would never see them again.

Was this that horrible 'beheading' nightmare, finally coming true? My mind was awash with faithless questions and fears. *Where could I run, where could I hide the boys? To run away now would be going against the government. I was already being charged with contempt of court; would they track us down and put me in jail? I would absolutely go to jail to protect Jon and Nick, but where and how could I hide them?* This was a devastating development. Terror-weighted tears ran down my face as I questioned the love and goodness of the Lord for the first time in a long time.

Was this to be the final result of all we had been through?

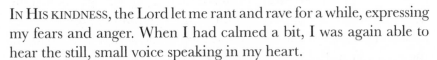

"Now we've got them," Blasphemy said with calm pleasure. *The courts are controlled by my master*, he mused, *and when that horrible woman returns with her sons, they will be trapped. I will make quick work of this assignment that has been so bungled by others.*

Blasphemy pulled himself upright and puffed out his chest. He looked almost human, indicative of his ranking high in the hierarchy. *Now we just must wait for the court date*, he thought. However, he figured it wouldn't hurt to go to her new home and have some fun terrorizing her. Apostasy wouldn't mind the intrusion on his territory, would he? *Of course not*, Blasphemy chuckled. *He is of lower rank than I, and he might enjoy some fun too.*

IN HIS KINDNESS, the Lord let me rant and rave for a while, expressing my fears and anger. When I had calmed a bit, I was again able to hear the still, small voice speaking in my heart.

The voice, full of love, said, "Remember that song you liked—the one about your life being in My hands?"

I had to stop and think. I guess God wasn't too disappointed in me for my outburst. *Thank you, God*, I thought. Then the song came to mind. Kathy Troccoli recorded it a few years before. The title was, "My life is in Your Hands". A few lines seemed highlighted in my memory:

> Sometimes I forget,
> and sometimes I can't see
> That whatever comes my way,
> You'll be with me.
> My life is in Your hands,
> my heart is in Your keeping.

I remembered those lyrics, and my tears fell for another reason.

"I am so sorry, Lord!" I said in prayer. "Please forgive me for not trusting You."

You are my beloved daughter. Go look at Isaiah 41:10 and 13, the Holy Spirit said gently in my head.

Reading it, I couldn't believe how much it helped me.

> So, do not fear, for I am with you; do not
> be dismayed, for I am your God. I will
> strengthen you and help you: I will uphold
> you with My righteous right hand. For I am
> the Lord your God who takes hold of your
> right hand and says to you, 'Do not fear, I
> will help you.'

WOW! God directly told me through His Word that I didn't need to worry. A note from Susan fluttered to the floor when I opened my Bible, Our time spent in her home at the beginning of the case was such a blessing. The blessings continued as the note reminded me of the verses from Joshua 1:5 and 9 (NIV):

> No one will be able to stand against
> you all the days of your life. As I was with
> Moses, so I will be with you; I will never
> leave you nor forsake you. Have I not
> commanded you? Be strong and courageous.
> Do not be afraid; do not be discouraged,
> for the Lord your God will be with you
> wherever you go.

I called Zach Taylor and left a message. He returned my call within an hour.

"I was expecting your call, Elizabeth. I received my official copies of the documents you received from the court."

"I was hoping you could continue to help us."

"Of course," he said in a reassuring tone.

"Do the boys need to come back with me?"

Now more severe, he said, "Unfortunately, yes. They must be available in case the judge asks to see them."

Once again, I began to make plans. Only now, I was no longer panicked. Though the trial was several months away, there was a lot to be done. Over the following weeks, Zach and I held conference calls. We tried, during that time, to forestall returning while discussing strategy if we did have to go through with the trial.

My attorney developed a file to give to the judge with the 'highlights' of previous hearings. He felt sure the judge would have a file from the court but wasn't sure if it would be complete. He also suggested I wear a dress that was solid blue. He called it the 'color of veracity.' The trial was only scheduled for one morning, as the judge didn't think more time would be needed.

Per Zach's instructions, I shopped and found a nice, conservative dress-royal blue with black trim.

I scheduled a meeting with my new boss to explain the situation and why I needed to take vacation days when I had just started the job. I gathered documentation, including some of my contemporaneous notes. I prayed a lot but didn't let on to Jon and Nick how serious the situation had become.

I called Detective Perry Johnson, along with my friends and prayer partners. Dr. Perez had already moved, leaving no forwarding address (very understandably)–so I collected some of his printed reports. I asked the Holy Spirit for guidance about what to bring because I couldn't take my whole file box with me. I wanted to be sure I would have precisely what was needed. My siblings (all out of state) were also very supportive with prayers and cash gifts.

Jim would pick us up from the airport, and we would stay with him and Brenda. We arrived on Sunday afternoon, ready for the trial to begin on Monday morning. And of course, Brenda would be on call with the boys as she had been many times before.

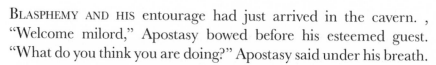

BLASPHEMY AND HIS entourage had just arrived in the cavern. , "Welcome milord," Apostasy bowed before his esteemed guest. "What do you think you are doing?" Apostasy said under his breath.

"I am here for a little fun, and I thought you might like to join me," Blasphemy said with a fiendish grin.

Apostasy was somewhat mollified and a little more interested. "What did you have in mind?"

"There is a human, new to your area, who caused no end of trouble in my area. We used to do trances on her, and her fear was truly mouth-watering and delightful."

Blasphemy conveniently left out the part of the story where she had learned to do serious battle and was not able to be troubled by the trances anymore. *Well,* Blasphemy thought, *This is a whole new battlefield, and an attack now would undoubtedly catch her off-guard.*

"All right," Apostasy agreed, "tonight as she goes to sleep."

ANOTHER BUSY DAY.

I reminded myself that this was the 'normal' life I had prayed for. "Thank You, Lord, for blessing us."

As I lay relaxing in my bed, an almost forgotten but familiar feeling came over me. It was a trance, only it was light and a very anemic grey color. *This isn't scary,* I thought as I immediately engaged in battle. *I can't believe they would try this again.*

It suddenly struck me as funny. I couldn't help it. I laughed out loud, and it was a joyous laugh. The attempted trance lifted right away, and it was the very last time they tried that.

THE UNDERLINGS, ALWAYS pawns in any battle and therefore, expendable, wailed and screamed all across the cavern. Blasphemy became annoyed and asked the nearest one, none too gently, "What in the world is wrong with you?"

The underling blathered, crying about something burning. Blasphemy couldn't understand what he was trying to say, which annoyed him further. He kicked the underling across the cavern and went to find Apostasy. Maybe he would know what all the racket was about.

When Blasphemy found him, Apostasy was also rolling around on the floor with his wings wrapped around him; screaming in pain. At that moment, Blasphemy became uncomfortably hot. His invisible wingtips burst into flame as intense pain exploded into his back. *'What is going on? He* thought as he crumpled over in pain. *She can't be laughing, is she?*

Being laughed at.

That was what set all the demons on fire, including him.

Blasphemy tried another attack and was rebuffed by more laughter. This time, blazing swords of the Enemy's angelic warriors followed the burning. In the heat of the ensuing battle, Blasphemy withdrew, returning to the relative safety of his own territory. He left the mess for Apostasy.

CHAPTER 30

OUR TRIP BACK was very smooth.
Though excited about flying and seeing their cousins, the guys were well-behaved and received pilot's wings from the flight attendant. And we really enjoyed our first evening back. Jim, Brenda, my nieces, and nephew reminisced about the times we went roller skating on Saturdays. We would drive from our old house to Jim's town, skate, and Brenda would fix lunch at their house afterward. Those Saturdays away from home allowed me my first sense of peace because I didn't have to be hypervigilant. We were safe under Jim's watchful eye, just like we were now.

"But I don't want to go to bed," Jon whined. For the boys, the excitement was wearing off and being replaced by fatigue.

Nick said, "Why do we have to go to bed?"

"First of all, because I said so. Second, your cousins have to get up for school tomorrow, and third, you are both tired. I can tell because you are whining. Let's go!"

How I wished this was just a vacation for all of us, and they could stay up late. But this was a serious 'errand'. Tomorrow, our entire future would be determined.

Jon and Nick went right to sleep after reassurances that they could play with their cousins when they got home from school. I, however, was not so successful going to sleep. I prayed, tossed and turned, and finally got up to read my Bible. I was reading Jesus' words in the gospel of Matthew when a section of print seemed to light up. I looked around to see where the light was coming from but couldn't detect an external source spotlighting the text.

It said:

> Are not two sparrows sold for a penny? [asked
> Jesus] Yet not one of them will fall to the ground
> outside your Father's care. And even the very hairs
> of your head are all numbered. So, don't be afraid;
> you are worth more than many sparrows. (Matthew
> 10:29-30 NIV – brackets mine)

I cried silently. *I know, Lord, but I am still frightened.*

I know, child, look again, He spoke to my heart.

As I looked at the page again, I saw another area of text light up. Matthew 10:19-20 read:

> But when they arrest you, do not worry about what
> to say or how to say it. At that time, you will be
> given what to say, for it will not be you speaking,
> but the Spirit of your Father speaking through you.

I felt cradled in God's arms and, after that confirmation, fell right to sleep.

The day of the trial dawned bright and sunny. I laid out the new outfits I had purchased for Jon and Nick in case they were called to come to court. I dressed carefully in the blue dress, black hose, and black pumps. *Humph...still a half-hour until Jim and I have to leave.* Nick and Jon were still asleep, so I opened my Bible again. A half-remembered verse tickled the edges of my mind. I had a feeling it was in Isaiah, so I flipped through the book of Isaiah and found it. It nearly jumped off the page.

> No weapon formed against you shall prosper, and
> every tongue which rises against you in judgment
> you shall condemn. This is the heritage of the

servants of the Lord, and their righteousness is from
Me," says the Lord. (Isaiah 54:17 NIV)

Wow. I suddenly felt calm and at peace all over. *Everything is
going to be alright. How is that possible?'* I wondered.

Then I remembered. Nothing is impossible for God.

Jim and I were pretty quiet on the ride to the courthouse. I was
still feeling a little fearful, but I had that underlying peace.

"Jim, I don't know how, but everything is going to be alright,"
I said out of the blue. He was a little startled since it was so quiet in
the truck.

"I hope so," he replied.

We rounded the last corner, and my stomach did its familiar
clench as the courthouse came into view. I reminded myself that
God had promised, *it's all settled, and you and the boys are free.*

Although we were in a different courtroom since the current
case was in domestic court, I took my usual spot next to my attorney.
Jim sat behind me in the spectator area. Grace, faithful as ever, sat
next to him. There was a bit of commotion when my ex-husband
and his attorneys arrived. My ex-father-in-law was present and
was insisting on a particular spot in the spectator area. He made a
woman already seated, move over even though there were plenty of
other seats. I would find out later why he did this.

The judge came in with a voluminous file, followed by his
clerk. The court reporter already sat at her small machine, ready to
transcribe the proceedings. The judge said, "This is a complicated
case, so I'd like to deal with the contempt citation first."

Greg's principal attorney jumped up, introduced himself and
his client, and said, "Mrs. Phillips left the state with the two minor
children in clear violation of the divorce decree. Social Services
dropped the case against my client, so there should be no protective
order in place, keeping him from seeing and interacting with his
sons. Mrs. Phillips has made that contact impossible by moving *four*

states away. She also callously refuses to send the boys by plane to visit their father." He sat down with a triumphant look on his face.

My attorney waited until he was called on by the judge. He stood and introduced himself and me. He was a real expert, concisely detailing the case over the last two years. The judge flipped through the case file as my attorney spoke. Greg's attorney objected strenuously multiple times, but the judge overruled him every time.

Finally, the judge glared at him, and he sat down.

Zach continued, showing there were confusing orders and serious concerns about the safety of the two children. He also mentioned that I had left my bank accounts open and a safe deposit box. My trip to help my elderly parents, as my dad had had several strokes, was extended, but I hadn't necessarily made a permanent move. The judge was quiet, studying the case file.

After what seemed like a long time, the judge spoke up.

"Mr. Phillips, I do not see that you have met the burden of proof for a contempt of court verdict," he started. "There is apparently no clear order in this case, so it was not violated. I do not find that Mrs. Phillips deliberately and flagrantly disobeyed court orders. She went to help her elderly parents with health issues. She also left open bank accounts and valuables in a safe deposit box, anticipating her return. I do not find Mrs. Phillips in contempt of court."

Greg snorted in disgust, and his attorney turned to him, telling him to be quiet.

And that, evidently, was that.

I had worried and stewed over this for months, but God already had it covered. I thanked the Holy Spirit for telling me to leave my bank accounts open. I never would have thought of that. It almost seemed to me that the judge was looking for a reason to vacate the contempt citation.

Looking at his watch, the judge seemed unhappy. "According to the docket, this hearing was to be completed in half a day. I'm not sure who scheduled it like that, but there is no way we will be finished today. Court is recessed until nine am tomorrow." He banged the gavel, picked up our giant file, and walked into his chambers.

I sat there in shock.

Another day of court?

Tomorrow?

I only brought one dress and our flight home left at seven-thirty pm tomorrow. The other side was surprised, too, though they were the ones who did the scheduling. I wondered if they had been over-confident about the outcome.

CHAPTER 31

WE ENJOYED ANOTHER evening with Jim, Brenda, and the kids. Jon and Nick were very concerned that I had to go back to court again the next day. My brain buzzed with anxious thoughts also, and sleep wasn't natural to come by. As I lay in bed, I prayed. I was so thankful that the contempt charge was dropped.

I heard the still, small voice say, "Check out Isaiah 25."

I was immediately enthralled when I read verse nine, which said,

> In that day, they will say, 'Surely this is our God;
> we trusted in Him and He saved us. This is the
> Lord, we trusted in Him; let us rejoice
> and be glad in His salvation.'

It made me think about another verse Grace had told me about. *Psalm 5? Was that it?* I wondered, wishing I had been better about memorizing Scripture. I looked it up and it was lit up from inside too. Psalm 5: 8-11 said,

> Lead me in the right path, O Lord, or my enemies
> will conquer me. Tell me clearly what to do and
> show me which way to turn. My enemies cannot
> speak one truthful word. Their deepest desire is
> to destroy others. Their talk is foul, like the stench
> from an open grave. Their speech is filled with

flattery. O God declare them guilty. Let them be
caught in their own traps. Drive them away because
of their many sins, for they rebel against You. But
let all who take refuge in You rejoice; let them sing
joyful praises forever. Protect them, so all who love
Your Name may be filled with joy.

The next morning in court, I wore the same dress, hose, and
shoes. That was all I brought.

The judge came in, once again toting the massive case file. He
set it down on his desk with a thump. The file's very size made me
think of all the trauma the boys had endured and my heart broke all
over again. I had to fight back the tears.

"I read a large portion of this file last night," the judge started.
"Fascinating reading," he said. I managed a little smile. "While
it is generally the position of the domestic court that children be
encouraged to be involved with both parents—"

I realized I was holding my breath.

"—I must say there are some very serious allegations included
here. I am a bit mystified at the action of the family court in this
case. Non-compliance with court orders is normally not a rationale
for dropping a case. But be that as it may, someone needs to take
responsibility for dealing with this difficult situation."

Turning to my ex-husband, the judge said, "Mr. Phillips, how
old are your sons?"

Obviously caught off-guard by the question, the boys' father
stammered before answering, "uh...three and four?"

The judge turned to me and said, "Is that correct Mrs. Phillips?"

"No, your honor, Jon is six, and Nick is five," I said. *I don't get it,*
I puzzled. *How could he not know that or at least subtract their birth year
from now? Maybe he can't even remember when they were born. He used to
have such a sharp mind.*

The judge moved on. "I have here a report from the intake social
worker. I am very impressed with what she says here. She states

that, in her sixteen years of intake experience, she has never seen two more frightened youngsters than these two boys. It is impressive because intake workers see a lot of trauma in their jobs." The judge looked directly at Greg.

I looked down at the table because tears threatened, and I was supposed to be concerned, but composed in my demeanor.

"Mrs. Phillips," said the judge. "Please step on up here to the witness box and be sworn in." I was startled to be called first. I was apprehensive of making a mistake, making things worse for the boys, having Greg yell at me, or irritating the judge. But I walked up with slow, calm steps and took the stand.

I placed my hand on a well-worn Bible and took the oath. "Please be seated," the judge said. As I sat in the witness box, it became blindingly clear why my ex-father-in-law had insisted on his particular seat again this morning. The way the courtroom was furnished, he had a direct line of sight to the witness stand. He was trying to be threatening and intimidating.

At first, I was a little rattled. Then I realized I could look at Jim or Grace instead, ignoring his stare. I settled back in the large, hard, wooden chair and tried to appear relaxed. *All I have to do is tell the truth,* I reminded myself. *Greg is the one who has to keep his lies straight.*

Just about that time, I had a sense that the Lord was standing behind me in the witness chair, invisible but immovable, with His hands on my shoulders. *What comfort!*

The female member of Greg's legal team stepped up to ask me some questions. As she did so, I realized I had nothing to fear, and I relaxed a bit.

"Do you have a boyfriend, Mrs. Phillips?" she asked.

I was taken aback, but I answered.

"No ma'am, I do not have a boyfriend, nor do I date," I stated, momentarily forgetting that I should answer only the question and not volunteer information.

"I find that hard to believe, Mrs. Phillips. Your divorce has been final for some time, has it not?"

"Yes, ma'am."

The judge broke in and said, "Do you have a point here?"

"Yes, your honor. Mr. Phillips contends that one of Mrs. Phillips' boyfriends abused his sons." she finished.

I was so shocked, I almost stood up. I couldn't believe what was being said here. Fortunately, my attorney jumped to his feet and registered an objection, so I didn't have to say anything right away. In another part of my brain, I thanked God that He hadn't sent my requested new husband.

Focus, Elizabeth! I warned myself.

I returned my attention to the courtroom as the judge sustained the objection, and the female attorney sat down. Now Greg's other attorney stood and glared at me.

"You have made some grave allegations about my client, Mrs. Phillips. How did you come up with those?"

"I wrote down anything the boys said that seemed strange or troubling to them."

"And just where are those notes now?'

"I have some examples right here."

My attorney warned me that this might happen, so I chose some of the contemporaneous notes that I felt I could afford to lose. I made copies, of course, but the originals were here in my hand. The notes were recorded on bank deposit slips, scraps of paper, on the backs of notes, sheets of paper from a class I had taken, my journal, or whatever I had handy at the time. The vast majority were in my file box at home but the selection I chose to bring was representative.

Suddenly, there was an outburst from Greg. He jumped up. "She just made those up," he sneered.

The judge shot him a warning glance. "Sit down, Mr. Phillips." To me, the judge requested, "May I see the notes please?" I handed the little pile to the bailiff and he gave them to the judge. The judge perused them carefully and said, "I believe these notes were recorded contemporaneously. There is one I find particularly upsetting."

Turning back to Greg, the judge said, "It seems that you forgot your younger son's birthday earlier this year, Mr. Phillips?"

"She was supposed to put them on a plane for my birthday, and we could have celebrated then," my ex-husband said lamely.

"When that did not happen, did you mail a card or a gift?" the judge inquired.

Greg looked sullen, and the judge said, "I asked you a question, Mr. Phillips."

Greg's attorney stared at him and poked him in the shoulder. He looked outraged and his attorney said, "It doesn't appear that anything was sent."

"That's a shame. Little boys love birthdays," the judge said, with a pensive note in his voice.

For another hour and fifteen minutes, I answered questions posed by Greg's attorney, the judge, and sometimes, clarification questions from my own attorney. Greg's legal team was insulting and demeaning. Zach was ready with reasonable objections when the primary lawyer on Greg's team stepped too far out of bounds. My ex-father-in-law continued to glare at me with threats in his eyes. By the end of my time in the witness stand, I was able to look him in the eye and not back down from his gaze.

I was glad when the judge said that I could 'step down,' but I wasn't at all sure if I had done all right.

Next, Zach called Dr. Pete, our pediatrician, to the stand. He was sworn in and answered questions about the boys' physical condition at the time of the initial allegations and his current notes. He noted neither one of the boys had grown physically in the year leading up to the initial revelations. I knew keeping horrible secrets to protect me was the main reason.

The other attorney began asking questions about why such young children would use anatomical names for body parts, like 'penis.' His contention was that the boys had been coached on what to say. Dr. Pete shut that down by saying, "In our practice, we advise parents to use the correct anatomical names for body parts because of sad situations where the children in an abuse case are called upon to testify. Their testimony is much more understandable than if they used 'cutesy' pet names for their affected body parts.

Dr. Pete stepped down, and the judge was quiet for several moments. "Mr. Phillips," he said, "you have the right to ask to have your sons here to answer questions." Greg looked at me.

"Mrs. Phillips, are the children available?" the judge asked.

"Yes, your honor. My sister-in-law can have them here in about 30 minutes." Even as I spoke, my heart stopped in my chest. I hoped to spare them from testifying and being cross-examined by Greg's attorney. It would not be pleasant for them and I had no idea what would happen.

There was a commotion at Greg's table again. My ex-husband had grabbed the arm of his leading attorney. It was clear he was telling him 'no' about bringing the boys to court. They began arguing in hushed tones at the table. Apparently, Greg wasn't going to take the stand either.

The judge called a twenty-minute recess, and we all trooped into the hall. I began feeling nauseous again, just thinking about what was happening. And what might be about to happen. Jim looked concerned, and only Grace was smiling. Twenty minutes until I would know what the rest of my life would look like.

The judge called us back into the courtroom. I was shaking, hoping it didn't show too much. He began by saying, "This was a very distressing case for everyone I am sure. My goal is that these children have a chance to heal and to know their dad."

My heart sank into my shoes. *Elizabeth Anne, don't you dare cry,* I told myself as sternly as I could manage. I didn't dare look at Jim, or Grace, or even my attorney. I was devastated and could only think, *Help us, Jesus!* I had to force myself to listen to the judges' instructions. He was talking again about the intact family unit and how important that was for children's healthy development whenever possible.

"Mrs. Phillips, you will involve the children in appropriate therapy with the goal of reunification of the father-son relationship if possible. No visitation currently, Mr. Phillips. When the therapist treating the boys agrees, you will call the boys every other week unless that causes undue stress on the boys. You will be involved in therapy yourself to discover what problems caused you to cease caring about your young sons' welfare. If I receive positive reports of progress from your therapist, we will reconvene to determine appropriate visitation.

"As to custody, I award sole legal and physical custody to Mrs. Phillips, and as such, she is free to live wherever she likes. Any questions?" He looked over to each one of us, "No? Court is adjourned."

Did he really just award me sole custody?

I wanted to ask somebody, but I looked at Jim's, Grace's, and my attorney's faces and realized he must have. I looked up at the wrong time and caught the glance of Greg. He looked furious, but even so, his eyes were just as dead as ever.

We gathered our things, anxious to be out of the courthouse so we could talk and celebrate.

Zach said, "I've never seen a case go like this. I didn't think sole custody was even an option, that's why I didn't seek it."

When I saw Greg and his father were far enough away, I threw my fist in the air and shouted, "Hallelujah!"

Jim said to me with a huge smile, "You said it would be okay, and it was! This really renews my faith!"

In the cavern, there was such confusion; a combination of terror and fury. Underlings and demons of all ranks were shoved, kicked, thrown, and jumping into the abyss. Screams of agony, horror, and anger filled the cavern as the master himself expressed his disappointment at losing his grasp on the two young boys he wanted.

GOD WINS!

In Him (Jesus) was life and that life was the light of all mankind. The light shines in the darkness and the darkness has not overcome it.

(John 1:4 NIV—parenthesis mine)

EPILOGUE

AFTER THE VICTORY in court, the boys and I flew home, and my heart was full of joy and thankfulness. We returned to our 'normal' life; work, school, and the boys' activities. After a time, we became involved with a great church and enjoyed the fellowship.

The guys grew up safe.

I still remained vigilant, though. For example, my dad picked the boys up at school each day. As time went by, I became less concerned about a kidnapping by the boys' father. We were all in therapy for a while and God did lots of healing in all three of us.

The criminal case against Greg and his associates went nowhere. There was one interesting thing that Detective Johnson mentioned in our last conversation. They were looking at a "person of interest" named Matt Ensero. *Was it possible that this was the Matt of 'Matt and Sara'?* I wondered. I thought, perhaps that could answer the confusion about whether "Matt and Sara" was one person or a man and a woman? *Another mystery unsolved.*

Jon and Nick did ask from time to time, why their dad and the others didn't have to go to jail for what they did to them and other children. I had no answer for them except to truthfully say that their dad's punishment was the worst I could imagine since he didn't get to know them or see them grow up.

Almost a decade later, the boys' father took us to court in Montana to try to get unsupervised visitation.

When Jon was eighteen and Nick seventeen, a supervised visit was arranged with a 'neutral' psychologist at his office. With lots of prayer, I put the guys back in therapy to prepare them for the visit. When we arrived at the appointed time at the office of the psychologist we did not know, I spoke to him briefly and went out to wait in my car. I felt a little anxious, but I fought back, in Jesus' Name, and felt peaceful knowing that God was in control.

About twenty minutes into the scheduled hour-long visit, Greg stormed out of the psychologist's office. He was enraged, but he just got in his rental car and left. I wondered what in the world had happened. Shortly thereafter, the two tall, not as blonde, guys emerged from the office with the psychologist chatting away. There were smiles all around. Things seemed to be calm, but my curiosity was eating me up from the inside out.

Finally, at long last, they came to the car.

"How are you doing, Guys?"

"We're fine" said Jon in his now deep voice.

"So, what happened?"

"He wanted us to come visit him and build a relationship, but we told him that we did not want to know him or have anything to do with him." Nick said with finality.

"He got very mad and stomped out," Jon said.

It was evident to me from their lack of anger and fear that God had indeed healed them.

My two sons have gone on to college, which they paid for themselves. One of them is married and they are both compassionate, generous, responsible adults.

God promised me that it was all settled, and the boys and I were free. As always, He keeps His promises!

ABOUT THE AUTHOR

ELIZABETH ANNE PHILLIPS-GLADSTONE has been writing for many years. The book you have just read is a novel based on a true story—her own.

Elizabeth currently resides in a small town in Montana. It is a lovely and quiet place, full of animals, especially dogs. In the winter, she enjoys mushing with a small team of her own dogs when she is not writing. Her children are grown, and she enjoys living simply with her husband and seeing her grandchildren.

It is her fondest desire that the reader of this novel be helped by the story and recognize the growth of Elizabeth's faith as it is available to anyone, as the story progresses. She is now free indeed.

RESOURCES

Child Help National Child Abuse Hotline: 1-800-422-4453

National Domestic Violence Hotline: 1-800-799-7233

Social Services (Child Protection Services) for your area:

www.childwelfare.gov/organizations...

Help from God: Pray. Anytime, anywhere.

The prayer of salvation (should you want it):
Dear Jesus,
Thank You for coming to earth to live and die for me. Your death on the cross was sufficient to cover all my sins, past, present and future. You rose from the dead to provide for my resurrection and my home is now in heaven. I ask you to be my Lord and my King forever. Help me to love You. In Jesus' Name, Amen.